In Defense of Reading

Blackwell Manifestos

In this new series major critics make timely interventions to address important concepts and subjects, including topics as diverse as, for example: Culture, Race, Religion, History, Society, Geography, Literature, Literary Theory, Shakespeare, Cinema, and Modernism. Written accessibly and with verve and spirit, these books follow no uniform prescription but set out to engage and challenge the broadest range of readers, from undergraduates to postgraduates, university teachers and general readers – all those, in short, interested in ongoing debates and controversies in the humanities and social sciences.

Already Published

In Defense of Reading: Teaching Literature in the Twenty-First Century

Daniel R. Schwarz

WILEY-BLACKWELL

A John Wiley & Sons, Ltd., Publication

This edition first published 2008
© 2008 by Daniel R. Schwarz

Blackwell Publishing was acquired by John Wiley & Sons in February 2007. Blackwell's publishing program has been merged with Wiley's global Scientific, Technical, and Medical business to form Wiley-Blackwell.

Registered Office
John Wiley & Sons Ltd, The Atrium, Southern Gate, Chichester, West Sussex, PO19 8SQ, United Kingdom

Editorial Offices
350 Main Street, Malden, MA 02148-5020, USA
9600 Garsington Road, Oxford, OX4 2DQ, UK
The Atrium, Southern Gate, Chichester, West Sussex, PO19 8SQ, UK

For details of our global editorial offices, for customer services, and for information about how to apply for permission to reuse the copyright material in this book please see our website at www.wiley.com/wiley-blackwell.

The right of Daniel R. Schwarz to be identified as the author of this work has been asserted in accordance with the Copyright, Designs and Patents Act 1988.

Library of Congress Cataloging-in-Publication Data

Schwarz, Daniel R.
  In defense of reading : teaching literature in the twenty-first century / Daniel R. Schwarz.
    p. cm.—(Blackwell manifestos)
  Includes bibliographical references and index.
    ISBN 978-1-4051-3098-1 (alk. paper)—ISBN 978-1-4051-3099-8 (pbk. : alk. paper) 1. English philology—Study and teaching (Higher)—United States. 2. Literature—Study and teaching (Higher)—United States. 3. Books and reading—Psychological aspects. I. Title.

PE68.U5S39 2008
801′.3—dc22
                                        2007052181

A catalogue record for this book is available from the British Library.

Set in 11.5/13.5pt Bembo by SPi Publisher Services, Pondicherry, India
Printed in Singapore by Utopia Press Pte Ltd

1   2008

For my wife, Marcia Jacobson,
my sons, David and Jeffrey Schwarz,
and in memory of my parents,
Florence (1916–2005) and Joseph Schwarz (1913–2004)

Also by Daniel R. Schwarz

Reading the Modern British and Irish Novel 1890–1930 (2005)

Broadway Boogie Woogie: Damon Runyon and the Making of New York City Culture (2003)

Rereading Conrad (2001)

Imagining the Holocaust (1999; rev. edn. 2000)

Reconfiguring Modernism: Explorations in the Relationship between Modern Art and Modern Literature (1997)

Narrative and Representation in the Poetry of Wallace Stevens: "A Tune beyond Us, Yet Ourselves" (1993)

The Case for a Humanistic Poetics (1991)

The Transformation of the English Novel, 1890–1930: Studies in Hardy, Conrad, Joyce, Lawrence, Forster, and Woolf (1989; rev. edn. 1995)

Reading Joyce's "Ulysses" (1987; centenary edn. 2004)

The Humanistic Heritage: Critical Theories of the English Novel from James to Hillis Miller (1986; rev. edn. 1989)

Conrad: The Later Fiction (1982)

Conrad: "Almayer's Folly" to "Under Western Eyes" (1980)

Disraeli's Fiction (1979)

As Editor

Damon Runyon: Guys and Dolls and Other Writings (2008)

The Early Novels of Benjamin Disraeli, 6 vols (consulting editor, 2004)

Conrad's "The Secret Sharer" (Bedford Case Studies in Contemporary Criticism, 1997)

Joyce's "The Dead" (Bedford Case Studies in Contemporary Criticism, 1994)

Narrative and Culture (with Janice Carlisle, 1994)

Contents

Preface

My contribution to the manifesto series is the result of my forty years of teaching and writing at Cornell, a few of which were actually spent as a visiting professor at other universities. Rather than an intervention into parochial academic debate, I seek to become part of a conversation about intellectual and cultural issues that concern serious readers and those interested in the state of the humanities at universities. I speak of how as a faculty member I see the evolution of the university and how as I scholar I see the changes in the discipline. In the hopes it will be helpful to others, I discuss what I do as a teacher and scholar. I offer some suggestions for those entering the field and discuss how to succeed once one has gained a professional footing. I imagine my audience to be not only those who teach or have taught literature in colleges and universities and those who are contemplating such a career, but also those who are interested in the way universities function and what they are trying to accomplish.

I. My Humanistic Credo

The following pages contain a vigorous defense of the kind of humanistic criticism I have argued for in my work and which forms the basic tenets of my teaching. I discuss my version of pluralism, think about the use and abuse of theory, argue for text-based readings and explain how I use historical contexts and theoretical material.

I believe that we can still evaluate literature in terms of its quality and importance. Even in an era when we read different texts in different ways, it is possible to return to a focus on primary texts. Concepts such as significant form, genre, persona, and structure are still definable in the Babel of critical discourses.

Let me state my credo: Literature is by humans, for humans, and about humans. The humanistic critic understands artists' lives in human terms rather than as superhumans of a different species, and realizes that there is a place for biography in understanding a writer's oeuvre. Humanistic critics believe in the importance of both the authors' conception of their subject and the choices they make in terms of technique, structure, and style because ultimately meaning depends on those choices. For humanistic critics, explaining literature is more important than self-dramatization of the critic's persona.

I believe that the close reading of texts—both from an authorial and resistant perspective—enables us to perceive more clearly; I believe in a continuity between reading texts and reading lives. I believe that the activity of critical thinking—not merely literary criticism—can be taught by the analysis of language. I believe in the place of the aesthetic. I believe that we can enter into imagined worlds and learn from them. Following Aristotle, I believe that the aesthetic, ethical, and political are inextricably linked.

What is my conception of valuable literary criticism? I believe that good criticism attends to the text, hears the narrator's voice, understands the author's artistry, differentiates between resistant readings and authorial readings, is aware of the process of reading and how it is different from the process of rereading. That is, good criticism is aware of both the initial encounter with a text and of rereading as well as how much a reread text impresses itself on the mind as memory. I recognize that there is no ideal reading and that reading is always somewhat a function of the reader's personality, social milieu, education, and historical moment. Good critics try to be observant and insightful, all the while being a bit self-conscious about how their own prejudices and preferences and how their own psyches and values give shape to their responses. Good critics do not become intoxicated with their own tastes and assumptions; indeed they have some humility, realizing that others may see things they do not and that criticism is an intervention within a community of inquiry, not an *ex cathedra* statement from a self-proclaimed guru. Good criticism does not revel in being dismissive of literary works or of other critics, and good critics take a deep breath before patronizing literary texts or condescending to other critics. Good criticism is written (or spoken) in lucid, accessible terms.

Our goal should be an empathetic reading of a text to discover the conscious and unconscious patterns of language that the author built into that text; those patterns convey a vision of how humans live to both the reading audience for whom the text was written and to the contemporary reader.

Literary criticism that addresses the experience of reading, respects the text and places the text in historical contexts can be quite wonderful, and we need be aware of what the methodological underpinnings are for such criticism. At the same time, in a maelstrom of fashionable academic garble, we must not lose the joys of reading and talking about literature. I do not believe literary studies advance teleologically in the way the study of DNA does or that our hypothetical theoretical models have the same truth possibilities as those of science. Sometimes we so want to be like our scientific brethren with advanced language and our own versions of terminology that we cut ourselves off from our natural audience—the community of serious readers within and without universities. Ironically modern science has at times been better at explaining itself than have literary fields, in part because some scientific terms playfully reach toward lucidity—quarks, string theory, red dwarfs and white giants, etc.—while some of our jargon deflects outsiders from understanding what we are doing.

Often we (or, rather, some segments of the community of literary scholars) invent pseudo-models that stay in fashion for a few years— sometimes leaving admittedly valuable remnants in their wake, sometimes not—and are replaced by new models. The great texts are less affected by these models than meet the eye and, in the hands of responsible critics, often the "new" readings are not very different from the "old." Thus many deconstructive readings were anticipated by such figures as William Empson, Kenneth Burke, and Northrop

Frye and, in the case of particular authors and texts, a host of other imaginative and careful readers. It does not denigrate current Marxist and postcolonial theorists to recall that their insights were anticipated not only by Michel Foucault and Fredric Jameson but also by Raymond Williams and Georg Lukacs.

If the field of literary studies is to prepare the next generation of secondary and college teachers as well as enrich the rest of our students and perhaps the community of serious readers, we need to preserve a healthy respect for close reading—with its emphasis on form—and to think about how language works in specific literary contexts. We need emphasize how literature reveals human motives and psyches through the intricacies of language.

In my writing and teaching, I live by two basic rules: "Always the text; Always historicize." While I have a healthy respect for what theory has taught us, I do not include "Always theorize" because theorizing is not a necessary and sufficient part of why we read. Theory can remove us, as James Soderholm has noted, "from both the pain and pleasure of human experience in its harrowing, earthy particularity" (Solderholm 1997, 7). My first mantra, "Always the text," leaves room for appreciating the felicities of language that render the particular and for responding to the aesthetic beauty of significant form. My other mantra, "Always historicize," includes understanding an artist within his historical and cultural context as well as being aware of the evolving responses that constitute the history of reading that writer. One meaning of historicism is not losing sight of the world beyond—what Frost called "the larger excruciations": hunger, poverty, war, tsunamis, and hurricanes—by simply focusing on the literary text as if it existed in a vacuum. I believe that there is at times a truth criterion for criticism; for example, some postcolonial theorizing about Africa ignores the actual conditions in today's Africa and is more propaganda than serious literary criticism.

In our critical inquiry, we need to answer basic questions: "Who is speaking to whom and why?"; "What is happening to the people within the imagined world of a text? What is their role in the narrated events and how do they affect, resist, or change the events?";

"What is the historical context?"; "What is the social and economic cause and effect within the imagined world?"; "How are human events affected by nature and fate?"; and "What artistic choices in terms of narrative or lyric presentation has the author made to realize that world?"

For me form has always been crucial for both aesthetic reasons and for what it does in terms of representation. The so-called new formalism is valuable because it makes us aware of how these choices shape our response and leaves room for discussing how the aesthetic generates pleasure in the reader even as it enables the reader to take on different identities in the imagined world and experience emotions—some painful—beyond his or her own life. We need not forget that the very reading of words may give us sensual pleasures—tactile, visual, and phonic.

Nor does one need abandon older forms of historicism to attend to formal aspects of literature. Indeed, as Erich Auerbach's formalism shows forms signify large historical patterns or, as Richard Strier puts it, for Auerbach "formal features of a text, [and] matters of style, can be indices to large intellectual and cultural matters" (Strier 2002, 211; also quoted in Levinson 2007, 565).

We need be aware of the difference between allowing a text to teach its readers how to read it, and using texts to bolster theoretical arguments and political positions. Put another way, I shall consider what I call the use and misuse of literary texts. Literary criticism necessarily depends on an awareness of what, in the transaction of reading, a particular reader does with a text, and we need be aware of how that transaction works when reading criticism.

I seek a pluralistic approach, which allows for multiple perspectives as well as a dialogic approach among those perspectives. I reject the view that pluralism is just another limited approach. Historicism is an important part of pluralism. Historicizing means taking into account: 1) the historical period in which the imagined events are being described; 2) the historical period of the reading audience for whom the work was written; and—although to a lesser extent—3) the historical period of the critics and readers whose responses we are reading or hearing.

Taking account of how readers and critics respond differently in different historical periods is what we call interpretive history and is another aspect of pluralism. The interpretative history of a text is a trialogue among: 1) the text as object which the original and subsequent critics write about and readers think about; 2) the subjective interests of all individual critics and ordinary readers; and 3) the predispositions and assumptions of the culture in which those original and subsequent critics write and readers live.

II. Teaching as a Humanist

Our role as humanists is to focus attention on what is special and distinct in the human enterprise. In my case that has ranged from studying and teaching the magnificent experimental works by Joyce, Conrad, and other modernists in literature and the visual arts, to, more recently, literary depictions of the horrors of the Holocaust. We need always remember that art is how we make sense of the world; literature is how we transform world into words and words into world. Literature and the other arts are a window onto who we were and who we are. In our reading and teaching, we need to strike a balance between addressing the ethical and political issues raised by artistic works and the forms by which those issues are presented. As a literature professor my focus is upon creativity, and as a cultural historian my focus is upon the historical and social contexts in which humans function.

My pleasure in being an academic derives not from chasing down rhetorical tropes, but from teaching students how to read carefully and perspicaciously, to think analytically and critically about why people speak and write as they do within and outside literary texts, to write lucidly and precisely, and to speak articulately and confidently. I feel pleasure when students fulfill their intellectual curiosity, widen the boundaries of their interests, learn to love the very texture of words, and become able to synthesize what they have learned—from texts and contexts—into cogent written and oral arguments, presentations, and constructions. Challenging students to think and write beyond the levels they thought they could and watching them succeed brings immeasurable satisfaction and makes me thankful every day that there is such a job as the one I have.

I began teaching at a time when many literature students and professors had an idealistic sense of mission and believed that reading the canonical texts carefully was a means to heighten students' awareness of the world around them, increase their ability to make moral discriminations, see themselves more clearly, and understand the behavior of others. Our work was important and not simply part of making a career or getting a professorship. My belief that great texts have gravitas, and that by understanding their subtleties and intricacies we learn from them, is still an important part of my passion for teaching literature.

Thus when we speak of how in Joseph Conrad's *The Secret Sharer*, a lonely, self-doubting man—who has been given great responsibility in his first appointment as captain—imagines that he has a great deal in common with a very different person, we expect students to understand that this is a process not unlike what young people—as a result of their own psychic needs—go through as they seek significant others and impute value to them.

We need teach our students how reading is an evolving process requiring attention to what the text is saying and not saying, to the structure of effects the text generates, and to how authors make conscious and unconscious choices to create their structures of effects. The pleasure of reading derives from our understanding a text's unity, that is, how the parts relate to the whole and in particular the consonance between beginnings and endings. In other words, when we teach the meaning of significant form we teach the form of significant meaning.

What can be more exciting than seeing a student develop enough confidence to challenge accepted ideas about how a text is read or to synthesize material from his courses in literature, philosophy and psychology into a coherent argument? Or to watch a young adult develop during his university years the ability to articulate his experiences and comment on cultural and political developments?

In the twenty-first century we teach in an age when we need to be sensitive to the complexity of a diverse student body, when the canon is both undergoing change and being challenged, when some professors are wedded to the literature of taking positions, and when political disagreement is defined as ideological resistance. I shall discuss how my teaching has evolved to include the relationship between literature and the visual arts and to include a richer understanding of parallels to and contexts from other cultures, including those in the Eastern world. I shall also discuss how teaching has changed in the computer age and at a time when we all do not have the same training or read the same literary canon. But these changes are challenges and my passion for teaching literature is unabated, and I am optimistic that great canonical texts will survive for the next generations of readers and teachers.

We also need to take pleasure in the joys of teaching and appreciate what we as teachers do. We live our professional lives among young people who are, for the most part, eager to learn and curious about books and ideas. We need to try to be aware of what they are doing beyond the classroom. We need to attend their musical and dramatic performances, read their writings in student newspapers and maga-zines, and even once in a while attend their athletic activities. When we give them the attention they deserve and listen carefully to what each is saying as an individual, they respond and often remember us throughout their own lives.

Where else but in a university could I watch young adults grow and participate in the process of that growth? I keep in touch with hundreds of my former students as an informal mentor and take a strong interest in their career development and their growth as partic-ipants and often as leaders in cultural and educational institutions as well as in national and international affairs. Watching this, too, is one of the pleasures of teaching. What can be more rewarding than to have scores of students visit and write to tell me how much I have meant to them? More than I deserve, students cite me as an influence.

Acknowledgments

I owe this book mostly to my experience of teaching and writing at Cornell these past 40 years and especially to my students from whom I have learned as much if not more than I have taught them. Even at a distance of many years, I am grateful to the participants in my five NEH summer seminars for college teachers and four NEH seminars for high school teachers.

I have learned a great deal from my continuing dialogue with Ron Ehrenberg, who knows more about the economics of universities than anyone I know and whose work is cited in the pages that follow.

Rather than single out all my colleagues in the English Department and other Cornell Departments, let me say it has been a privilege to teach in the same department as M.H. Abrams, Laura Brown, Jonathan Culler, and the late Anthony Caputi as well as with such former colleagues as Phillip Marcus and Michael Colacurcio.

I have been privileged to work with Blackwell's Emma Bennett and Hannah Morrell. Among the fine Cornell English department staff, I have enjoyed working especially with Vicky Brevetti, Robin Doxtater, and Darlene Flint.

My wife Marcia Jacobson is my best friend as well as a generous, demanding, and insightful reader and editor from whom I learn every day.

1

The Odyssean Reader or the Odyssey of Reading: "Of Ourselves and of Our Origins"

I. Reading as an Odyssey

I shall be writing about happens when we read or what I call the odyssey of reading, and I shall be doing so in terms of what for me has been my own exciting odyssey of reading. I write not only as a literary scholar but as a lifetime reader inquiring into why we read, and like Odysseus, who learned a great deal from his wanderings, I hope I offer something from my long experience.

What exactly is reading but the journey of the mind to understand a world beyond itself? While we need think about what happens when we read any kind of text or go to a film or a concert—or come to terms with a painting in a museum—my concern is with imaginative literature and what we do when we read that literature and how that relates to how we teach literature.

Two of my passions are travel and reading and they have much in common. It happens one of the genres in which I myself have recently been writing is travel-writing and I want to apply that genre to this discussion. Our experience through a text is a kind of journey. What I mean by my title is that a journey through texts is always a journey we share with authors, but it is also one we take alone. With their complexities and traps, their seeming interpretive solutions undermined by further problems, their potential for leading us astray, arresting our progress with puzzling moments, and their capacity for opening our eyes, these journeys are odysseys.

Complex texts that present difficulties and frustrations, texts such as *Moby Dick* and *Ulysses*, tend to make reading a journey with setbacks and challenges. Like the protagonist undergoing the quest, we are often buffeted about and need to stop frequently, particularly when these texts are long, but when we pick up the text we resume our journey. The destination of our odyssey of reading—the conclusion of the journey as we reach home—is the moment when we close the text after its last word. But, in a sense, that is also the beginning of another odyssey, namely the odyssey of reflection. When we complete a major odyssey of reading, we know that reading is a way we come to know ourselves.

We need think of our readings as odysseys with their own beginnings and endings or, in contemporary terms with their own take-offs and landings, departures and arrivals. When we begin a book, we seal ourselves off from other worlds, just as when we take a trip to a different society. As I wrote in one of my published poems entitled "Travel:"

Travel

is for me hermetic,
an ordering: each trip
a life, with its own defined
beginning and ending,
an escape from
thick textures
of adult life—heavy weights
of work and relationships.
Travel is world
out of time:
anxieties controlled,
mortality put off,
attention distracted.
Trip is oasis,
an abbreviated lifetime,
sealing world

> from intrusion,
> creating space
> of two spare,
> bare weeks.

If I change the words "travel" and "trip" to reading, wouldn't we have an apt description of what we do as readers? Each of our reading odysseys is different, just as no two people take the same trip to India even if they are on the same tour, or make the same trip to Paris even if they sleep in the same bed. I grew up in a world where we pretended that if we as a seminar or a group of colleagues talked about a book enough our readings would be close to the same, but we now know that each of us brings our own prior experience—reading and otherwise—and our own psyche and values to our odyssey of reading.

Reading is a kind of travel, an imaginative voyage undertaken while sitting still. Reading is immersion; reading is reflection. Reading takes us elsewhere, away from where we live to other places. We read to satisfy our curiosity about other times and places, to garner information about what is happening in the world beyond our lives, to gather the courage to try new things even while considering admonitions not to try dangerous ones, and to learn about experiences we might try in the future. Our reading helps formulate narratives—of personal hopes, plans, putative triumphs—that help us both to understand our pasts and to make plans for our futures. As Wallace Stevens put it in "The Idea of Order at Key West," words enable us to discover "ourselves and our origins" and perhaps to experience what Stevens calls "ghostlier demarcations" and "keener sounds" than we may find in our own lives.

We read for information that we need and seek. We read because we are curious and wish to learn other ways of organizing life not only in our own culture but also in others. We read to supplement our life experience, and that surely includes reconfiguring the values we are taught. When reading, we extend our horizons; we come to understand what it is like to be of a different gender, race, and class, to have a different psyche. We read for company when we are lonely, for solace when we are in pain, and to recuse ourselves from the painful, sad and lonely world we at times live in—a world that can be fraught with political and personal problems. We read, paradoxically, to rest from the slings and arrows of outrageous fortune and the challenges of our lives as well as to become more alert to those challenges.

We read not only to alleviate pain but also for amusement. We read to relax from the pressures and pleasures of our everyday world. We read also to delight ourselves, to vicariously share pleasures, joys, sensuality, and passion. Reading, we must not forget, is also a kind of play. We read to enjoy the pleasure of words, their sensuality and materiality, the smells and tastes and visions they evoke, the desires they elicit, the laughter as well as the tears and even physical disgust and pain they arouse.

To be sure, some reading can be complex and difficult, requiring an effort beyond that of watching TV or even scanning the Internet. For example, Holocaust narratives or novels, or memoirs about growing up black in America, take us into worlds that fascinate us and that give breadth and depth to our emotional lives, but from which we may be glad to return to our own world. What each of us finds painful varies, for each of us reads differently depending on our experience.

We need recognize continuity between reading imaginative and non-imaginative literature. We can never afford to be either passive detached readers or, alternatively, completely empathetic readers who suspend our judgment when listening to or reading speeches from our political leaders or reading articles in the *New York Times*. Even when we read to seek information we are aware whether the text is well organized or flaccid, efficiently succinct or prolix, lucid or opaque, whether logically argued or simply asserting what its author wants us to believe. And we need to discover the author's own underlying assumptions, idiosyncrasies, and perhaps biases.

Different readers will have different responses depending on their reading and life experience. As postmodernists we are skeptical, suspicious, and even cynical readers because we frequently see truth claims made for texts—truth claims that prove to be false, whether it be George W. Bush's claims of weapons of mass destruction in Iraq, or exaggerated claims of truth by supposed memoirists. We become wary readers and at times take on the role of detectives. An experienced reader of Holocaust texts should have been suspicious of Binjamin Wilkomirski's supposed Holocaust memoir, *Fragments*— which I suspected because of its excesses as being a fraud even when it was winning awards—especially if the reader knows about the history of Jerzy Kosinski's *The Painted Bird*, an early Holocaust fiction that originally was presented as autobiography.

We also read to confirm who we are, even as we think we are reading to supplement who we are. Certainly women writers and readers respond differently than men to Virginia Woolf's discussion of a woman writer's needs in *A Room of One's Own* or to Mrs. Dalloway's being reduced to a kind of social adjunct to her husband's life, but I, too, can understand Mrs. Dalloway's loneliness, her fears of death, and the irony of her social triumph at the novel's final party.

Optimists can find reinforcement for their views in William Wordsworth's joy in life. Self-help books can help restore physical health and esteem. Religious books can help give the disorder of life some order. Depressives can find reinforcement in reading about other depressives or by reading writers who believe, like Thomas Hardy, that, all things being equal, things will turn out badly. Reading can do damage by pushing psychopaths, sociopaths, and even severely depressed people over the edge. Well-read suicides have cryptically quoted passages from literature in their last notes; one well-known scholar is reputed to have included in his suicide note famous lines from *King Lear* (V.ii.9–13):

> Men must endure
> Their going hence, even as their coming hither;
> Ripeness is all.

Perhaps we all need be wary of such overly empathetic reading.

Reading, we know, enables an informed citizenry and sometimes creates a misinformed one. Certainly information about the Vietnam War, the scandal that became known as Watergate, the non-existence of weapons of mass destruction in Iraq raised the consciousness of

Americans. Knowing about how humans lived in the recent and ancient past helps us understand who we are and how to proceed. Reading about the Holocaust and slavery helps shape our ethical sensitivity.

Mark Edmundson writes in "The Risk of Reading":

> The best way to think about reading is as life's grand second chance. All of us grow up once; we pass through a process of socialization [...]. Yet for many people, the process of socialization doesn't quite work. The values they acquire from all the well-meaning authorities don't fit them. And it is these people who often become obsessed readers [...]. They read to be socialized again, not into the ways of their city or village this time but into another world with different values. Some people want to revise, or even to displace, the influence their parents have had on them. (2004, 11–12)

As reader, critic, teacher, and poet, I would subscribe to James Wood's idealistic view of the implicit contract between artist and reader:

> [W]hat I am most interested in is what we might nebulously call human truth—a true account of the world, as we experience it, and of the full difficulty of being in that world. Creating living characters, and writing fiction expressing what Henry James called "the present palpable intimate" entails, for me at least, some kind of morality. Requiring readers to put themselves into the minds of many different kinds of other people is a moral action on the part of the author. (2004, D3)

I would extend Wood's remark to apply to poetry, drama, and perhaps even serious non-fiction.

My codicil to Wood's Leavisite focus on bracing moralism and tangible realism would be that we need to remember that such terms as "human truth," "authenticity," and "knowledge" mean different things to different people and that the largest community of readers is one. W.H. Auden's line, "'O Where are you going?' said reader to rider" with a pun on writer reminds us that the writer is a guide but that each reader undertakes his own journey ("The Three Companions").

Indeed, the rider (writer) in frustration with a probing and resistant interlocutor—that is, the reader—would banish the reader from his premises ("'Out of this house'—said rider to reader").

Reading is a dialogue between reader and writer; readers bring their imaginations, memories, thinking processes, moral and social values, historical knowledge, and prior experiences to every text. Verlyn Klinkenborg, in an Editorial Observer piece in the *New York Times* entitled "Reading Thackeray's 'Vanity Fair' with the Illustrations Intact," (August 30, 2004, A18) perceptively remarks: "Good readers, of course, bring the kinetics of imagination to the text. And compared with the genuine collaboration that exists between readers and a writer, the dynamism of hypertext, for instance, looks preposterously mechanical."

He rightly cites the intrusive voice of *Vanity Fair* manipulating his fictional puppets as an example of this collaboration: "Thackeray met his readers more than halfway. He is an interlocutor in his novel as much as its narrator. He patrols the scenes of 'Vanity Fair'—London high and low, the battle of Waterloo, the prosperous ducal town of Pumpernickel—happy to intervene when a point needs clarifying, eager to field readers' comments even as the novel is unfolding" (A18). Whether we consider William Makepeace Thackeray's wonderful illustrations to be the work of the narrative voice or that of an illustrating presence outside the text, we can agree with Klinkenborg's comments on the dialogue between Thackeray's texts and illustrations: "They pop up with the lightness of touch, the glibness, that characterizes Thackeray as a writer at his best. They are comments, often ironic, on the pictures developing in a reader's mind."

But we need keep in mind that there are many other kinds of collaboration between author and reader. The collaboration between author and reader can be one in which the author invites the reader to share his views of an unreliable imperceptive narrator as in James Joyce's "Araby" or, more flagrantly, Edgar Allan Poe's "The Tell Tale Heart." In "Araby," Joyce expects us to see what the narrator, slightly older than the younger self whose experience of frustrated desire and religious guilt is the subject of the story, does not see—namely that he is locked into a Catholic epistemology that confines him and that he is prone to hyperbolic responses—on occasion rendered in purple prose—reflecting his youth.

A resistant reader, while acknowledging Joseph Conrad's 1899 version of passionate anti-colonialism when *Heart of Darkness* was written, may still refuse to collaborate in what now seems Conrad's racist or sexist views in *Heart of Darkness.* The reader may join Chinua Achebe (1977) in realizing that not only is Conrad's critique of imperialism woefully incomplete, but he may, remembering how important exposing King Leopold II of Belgium's imperialism was to European history, forgive Conrad for not being fully aware of the implications of that critique in terms of our understanding of racism. While Kurtz's nationality is never specified and the British are spared from Conrad's condemnation, *Heart of Darkness* is a visionary text that awakened the world to King Leopold II's exploitation of the Congo and, by implication, colonial imperialism.

We need to think, too about how we visualize when we read. I myself do not have a full photographic picture when I read unless I dream about the novel, but I know other readers are more visual. Thus my imagination of a novel like *Vanity Fair* is as cognitive and reflective as it is visual if not more so. How many people remember the color details of clothing in a realistic novel? What more of us remember is the social and moral dimensions of character, the personality of characters, how they speak, the presence and tone of the narrative voice, and the broad outlines of setting—especially the qualities emphasized, like the fog of *Bleak House,* and the gloomy nighttime of *The Secret Agent.*

II. The Continuity between Reading and Writing

By citing one of my own poems—and, while I have published 65 or so poems, I have no illusions that my own poetry is more than a drop in the literary ocean—I am suggesting a continuity between reading and writing.

I think most imaginative writers write primarily when they need to delve into their psyches and discover who they are and, secondarily but still importantly, when they need share the results of that process with others. They—we—use words to understand ourselves and the world we live in. Let me turn to the Turkish 2006 Nobel Laureate Orhan Pamuk on the role of the writer in transforming words from real life into imagined worlds:

> A writer is someone who spends years patiently trying to discover the second being inside him, and the world that makes him who he is [...]. To write is to transform that inward gaze into words, to study the world into which we pass when we retire into ourselves, and to do so with patience, obstinacy, and joy. [...] But once we have shut ourselves away we soon discover that we are not as alone as we thought. We are in the company of the words of those who came before us, of other people's stories, other people's books—the thing we call tradition. (2007, 82–3)

What I find striking in these eloquent words is how they describe the activities not only of the writer but also of the reader. Let me revisit these passages, substituting the word reader for writer, to stress how the reader, too, is engaged in the introspective, imaginative quest— odyssey if you will—for understanding:

> A *reader* is someone who spends years patiently trying to discover the second being inside him, and the world that makes him who he is [...]. To read is to transform that inward gaze into words, to study the world into which we pass when we retire into ourselves, and to do so with patience, obstinacy, and joy. [...] But once we have shut ourselves away we soon discover that we are not as alone as we thought. We are in the company of the words of those who came before us, of other people's stories, other people's books—the thing we call tradition. I believe literature to be the most valuable tool that humanity has found in its quest to understand itself. (2007, 83)

When we read we descend into ourselves, not unlike writers. If I may return to Pamuk:

> I believe literature to be the most valuable tool that humanity has found in its quest to understand itself [...]. For me, to be a writer is to

acknowledge the secret wounds that we carry inside us, wounds so
secret that we ourselves are barely aware of them, and to patiently
explore them, know them, illuminate them, own them, and make them
a conscious part of our spirits and our writing. (2007, 83, 90)

Doesn't reading also discover the deeply buried self—the fixations
and obsessions, the dark memories, the pain we barely recognize, what
Pamuk calls the "secret wounds"—and create a persona different from
our everyday social self?

My point is that the reader's odyssey mirrors that of the writer and
we read not only to complement our experience, but also to discover
who we really are. When we read fully and passionately and with rapt
attention, do we not discover our secret selves, and probe deeply into
our psyches? Let me return to my last Pamuk quotation and once
again make my substitution of reader for writer:

For me, to be a *reader* is to acknowledge the secret wounds that we
carry inside us, wounds so secret that we ourselves are barely aware of
them, and to patiently explore them, know them, illuminate them,
own them, and make them a conscious part of our spirits and our
reading. (2007, 90)

What I am arguing is that we overestimate the distinction between
reader and writer. I think an active, passionate, imaginative reader
responds to words with joy, and it is not surprising that many of our
great writers—Jorge Luis Borges, T.S. Eliot, Stevens, and Joyce—are
also perspicacious readers. Joyce understood the continuity of reading
and writing when he has the jejune Stephen Dedalus think, in the
opening line of the third episode of *Ulysses*, "Signatures of all things
I am here to read." We might note that the third episode is appropri-
ately called "Proteus" to emphasize how Stephen needs discover how
words are transformed into worlds.

Readers and writers share a belief in language and a belief that if
we can only find the right words, we can communicate. They believe
in the capacity of the human mind to understand, and believe, despite

all our failings, that we need others—family, friends, community—and that words are essential to the way we connect to others.

Who is a serious reader? A serious reader is a person for whom literature—imaginative as well as serious non-fiction—matters, and for whom literature is not simply something to be skimmed as a pre-text for finding ideas for essays and conversations but rather as an opportunity to enter empathetically into—depending on the text—the author's imagination, memory, value system, historical milieu, and, indeed, his way of being present at a particular time and place.

When we enter as odyssean readers into an imagined world, we become involved with what Nadine Gordimer has called "the substance of living from which the artist draws his vision," and our criticism must speak to that "substance of living" (Gordimer 1981, n.p.). In Third World and postcolonial literature—and in politically engaged texts such Elie Wiesel's *Night* or Primo Levi's *The Periodic Table*—this involvement is particularly intense. Thus the interest in postcolonial and Third World literature—perhaps accelerated by Wole Soyinka's and Derek Wolcott's Nobel prizes—challenged some tenets of deconstruction. Literature written at the political edge reminds us what literature has always been about: urgency, commitment, tension, and feeling. But at times have we not transferred those emotions to parochial critical and theoretical debate among ourselves rather than to our responses to literature?

While it may not be completely irrelevant to talk about gaps, fissures, and enigmas and about the free play of signifiers in the poetry of Wally Serote ("Death Survey") and Don Mattera ("Singing Fools"), we must focus, too, on these authors as persecuted blacks in the former regime of South Africa, and the pain and alienation that they felt in the face of persecution. Nadine Gordimer has written—and Joyce might have said the same thing about Ireland—"It is from the daily life of South Africa that there have come the conditions of profound alienation which prevail among South African artists" (Gordimer 1981, n.p.).

When discussing politically engaged literature—be it Soyinka, Gordimer, Wiesel, or Levi—we need to recuperate historical circum-stances and understand the writer's ordering of that history in his imagined world. We need to know not merely what patterns of provisional representation are created by language but the historical, political, and social ground of that representation. We need to be open to hearing the often unsophisticated and unironical voice of pain, angst, and fear.

III. Reading as a Culture

What we read as a culture tells us who we are as American people and is therefore an ingredient of cultural studies. What various communities read—whether ethnic, professional, social communities, academic departments, reading clubs—helps define that group's values and identity. What we read in an academic format tells us, at a particular moment in time, what kind of university or department we are or wish to be. Various ethnic and religious subgroups read different books. Cultural conflict is often enacted in a battle of the books.

Reading makes us better citizens. What we read in biography, history, and fiction not only teaches us about diverse politicians and their illusions, delusions, accomplishments, and vanity, but also enables us to see cultural conflict. We want to see how the minds of others work—authors and their subjects—and what values they live by. In a puzzling world where statesmen and leaders do not say what they mean, we wonder if they even know what are lies; in any case, we read as part of our quest to understand. Whether a poem or a novel or an Op-Ed piece, we read to supplement our experience, modify who we are, and, if we are moved or touched, perhaps reconfigure our beliefs and feelings.

What each of us reads individually tells us who we are in terms of our own separate and special identity. We define ourselves by what we read and what we choose not to read—our desires, our needs, our demands, our disappointments, our fixations, our obsessions.

Bestseller lists—including self-help books, books about successful investing as well as books about dieting, health and aging, fashion, political autobiography, celebratory hagiography—open a window on who we are and who we expect to be. We enjoy learning about the lives of the rich and famous—the restaurants they eat at, their galas, and the gossip about their love-life—even while clinging to a democratic vision and belief in meritocracy. Among other things, the books we read and films we see show that we want a world of ethnic diversity and choices, yet we don't want to abandon certain Rockwellian myths of what America was.

While there are notable exceptions and serious reading groups, most reasonably literate Americans—indeed, former university students—spend a good deal of their fiction reading time on page-turners such as Dan Brown's *The Da Vinci Code* rather than dense texts like the Portuguese Nobel laureate's José Saramago's *The History of the Siege of Lisbon*. Even erudite academics read fiction—mysteries, science fiction—for a good story and escapism.

A survey released a few years ago by the National Endowment of the Arts ("Reading at Risk: A Survey of Literary Reading in America," June 2004) showed that reading for pleasure had declined in the United States. Paradoxically, the survey shows that readers are more active participants in the community—more likely to perform volunteer and charity work, to go to museums and concerts, and to attend sporting events than non-readers. In an Op-Ed piece in the *New York Times* entitled "The Closing of the American Book," Andrew Solomon contends:

> There is a basic social divide between those for whom life is an accrual of fresh experience, and those for whom maturity is a process of mental atrophy. [...] You are what you read. If you read nothing, then your mind withers, and your ideals lose their vitality and sway [...]. We need to teach people not only how, but also why to read. The struggle is not to make people read more, but to make them *want* to read more. (2004, 17)

If we agree with Solomon that reading opens the doors and windows of our minds to fresh experience, isn't our challenge as teachers to take part in a spirited defense of the joys of serious reading? We read to see how the world looks from other points of view and to complement our own limited experience. We read to enter in other places and time, to transport ourselves into a different world as if on a magic carpet. As postmodernists desperately trying to know others, we read to overcome our fears of unknowability—that we cannot know others and others cannot know us.

A community of readers engaged with serious books becomes, as individuals respond to the book and define its cultural and individual meaning, a community of inquiry. This takes place for canonical texts and serious bestsellers such as Al Gore's book on global warming entitled *An Inconvenient Truth*.

IV. What Is Literary Meaning? Responding to and Resisting the Author's Values

Literary meaning depends on a trialogue among: 1) authorial intention and interest; 2) the formal text produced by the author for a specific historical audience; and 3) the responses of a particular reader in a specific time. Literary texts mediate and condense anterior worlds and authors' psyches. The condensation is presented by words, words that are a web of signs that signify something beyond themselves; within a text, words signify differently. Some words and phrases almost summon a visible presence; others are elusive or even may barely matter in the terms of representation—as in Joyce's encyclopedic catalogues in "Cyclops."

The context of any discourse determines the meaning—or should we say the epistemological and semiological value of the word or sentence? And once we use the word "value," are we not saying that words have an ethical quotient? Human agency—on the part of author, reader, or characters within real or imagined worlds—derives in part from will, from the idiosyncrasies of human psyche, and, in part, from cultural forces beyond the control of the individual. This is another way of saying that language is constituted and constituting, although it gives subjective human agency to the act of constituting. While we need, as resistant readers, to be alert to the implications of racist, sexist, classist, and anti-Semitic nuances, we also need to stress reading the words on the page in terms of the demands made by the text's context and form—in particular, by its structure of effects or what I have called the Doesness of the text.

If awareness of oneself and one's relationship to family and community—including one's responsibilities, commitments, and values—is part of the ethical life, then reading contributes to greater self-understanding. Reading complements one's experience by enabling us to live lives beyond those we live and experience emotions that are not ours; it heightens our perspicacity by enabling us to watch figures—tropes that are personifications of our fellow humans—who are not ourselves, but like ourselves.

Rather than being divorced from life, our reading experience, if we read actively and with intelligence, is central to life and contributes to the development of the mature personality. Literature provides surrogate experiences for the reader, experiences which, because they are embodied within artistically shaped ontologies that shape our responses by means of their structure of effects, heighten our awareness of moral discriminations. Yet, I suggest, what distinguishes literature from moral philosophy is literature's specificity, its nominalism, and its dramatized particularity.

Literature raises ethical questions, ones that enable us to consider not only how we would behave in certain circumstances, but also whether—even as we empathetically read a text—we should maintain some stance of resistance by which to judge that text's ethical implications. While some artistic experiences allow more of a moral holiday than others, even abstract art finally needs to be recuperated in human terms and thematic issues. Literature calls upon us to respond fully, viscerally, with every dimension of our psychological and moral being.

Let us turn to an example where literature demands a response. When T.S. Eliot's speaker in the first verse paragraph of his dramatic monologue "Gerontion" (1920) derides in most derogatory terms "the jew"—drawing upon a rhetoric of insult to milk the stereotype of the Jew—we respond in multiple ways:

> I was neither at the hot gates
> Nor fought in the warm rain
> Nor knee deep in the salt marsh, heaving a cutlass,

15

Bitten by flies, fought.
My house is a decayed house,
And the jew squats on the window sill, the owner,
Spawned in some estaminet of Antwerp,
Blistered in Brussels, patched and peeled in London.
The goat coughs at night in the field overhead;
Rocks, moss, stonecrop, iron, merds.
The woman keeps the kitchen, makes tea,
Sneezes at evening, poking the peevish gutter.

Devoting three lines to derogate the landlord with onomatopoeic verbs and participles—"squats," "spawned," "blistered," "patched," and "peeled"—is a gross example of the rhetoric of insult, prejudice, and defamation. Jews are not only associated in the passage with disease and decay, but with lust and defecation. We stop and consider what this tells us about the narrator, whether we can attribute the words to an imperceptive speaker, whether the author is ironic, whether the narrative of modernism adequately takes account of Eliot's anti-Semitism, whether a formal analysis that ignores a critique of the early twentieth century cultural context in which such language was permissible and even acceptable, and, finally, whether the focus on formalism caused critics of the next several decades after publication to ignore the inflammatory nature of this image—despite the Holocaust.

Texts demand ethical responses from their readers in part because *saying* always has an ethical dimension and because we are our values and we never take a moral holiday from our values. We can no more ignore the ethical implications of what we read than we can ignore the ethical implications of life. But how does one discuss how one reads ethically (and how do we teachers bring that ethical dimension into our classroom) without imposing our own values? Ethical questions have usually focused on character behavior in prose fiction and drama, but clearly seduction lyrics such as Andrew Marvell's "To His Coy Mistress" or megalomaniac pronouncements such as that of the speaker of Robert Browning's "My Last Duchess" raise issues about the speaker's human behavior that need be addressed.

V. Why We Read

We read to discover the conscious and unconscious patterns of language that the author built into a text because those patterns usually convey a vision of how humans live. We should read literature as an imagined representation of historical events and human behavior. Human behavior is central to most works and should be the major concern of analysis. Thus a major interest to readers is in how imaginary people behave—what they fear, desire, doubt, need—imaginary including poetry and drama as well as novels and stories. Although modes of characterization differ, the psychology and morality of characters need to be understood as if they were real people; for understanding others like ourselves helps us to understand ourselves. Even the seeming exceptions prove the rule: complex plots enact and represent human actions; descriptive poems reflect the perspective of an observer.

We need always remember that literary works are by humans, about humans, and for humans. A place is once again being cleared for literary criticism informed but not driven by theoretical hypotheses. Such criticism necessarily will emphasize modes of narration and representation. Literary criticism necessarily depends on an awareness of what, in the transaction of reading, a particular reader does to a text. We need a pluralistic approach, which allows for multiple perspectives and a dialogic approach among those perspectives. Such a criticism leaves room for resistant readings—feminist, ethnic, and gay—without allowing the text to be appropriated by theoretical or political agendas. It means teaching our students that reading is an evolving process requiring attention to what the text is saying, to the structure of effects the text generates, and to how authors make conscious and unconscious choices to create their structure of effects.

VI. Interpretive History and Meaning

Let us think about how interpretive history affects the meaning of a text. An aesthetics of reading needs account for changes in the way we read an author; this is what we call interpretive history. In a sense, a text changes even though the author writes no more words. The interpretative history of a text—which is different from its meaning—depends on three factors: 1) the text as an object which critics write about; 2) the subjective interests of individual critics; and 3) the predisposition and assumptions of the culture in which those critics write. The interpretive history of a text is the history of its odysseys of reading as shaped by culture but also by the critics. The value of the theoretical revolution has been that it created new odysseys of reading, although at times it distracted us from the text as an ontology—what I call its Isness—and from how a text creates through the process of reading particular responses—the Doesness of the text as opposed to its Isness. But at its best the theoretical explosions created new maps of reading that have guided us on different journeys.

The literary canon enriches itself because each generation brings something different to major authors and texts. As my teaching has evolved in response to changes in literary and cultural perspectives, the texts that I teach have changed as well.

Let me cite an example of how the odyssey of reading a canonical text has changed. Until 1980 few critics thought about the homoeroticism of the male bonding in Conrad's *The Secret Sharer*. Now it is a foregrounded subject. Thus, in my edition of *The Secret Sharer* in the Case Studies in Contemporary Criticism series, every contributor—James Phelan, Bonnie Kim Scott, Michael Levenson, J. Hillis Miller, and myself—took up the subject in one way or another. I now also see *The Secret Sharer* in the context of other works which focus on seeing and being seen, including Henry James's *The Turn of the Screw* and Thomas Mann's *Death in Venice*, and trace that focus back to the seminal nineteenth-century painter, Édouard Manet, and especially his *Déjeuner sur l'herbe*. While I have always read *The Secret Sharer* as a confessional psychodrama requiring psychological and at times a Freud-based psychoanalytic criticism, the insights of Jacques Lacan on the gaze also play a role in my current response. Finally I see continuity between *The Secret Sharer* and other novels of bachelor figures at the turn of the century, a period that regarded bachelors with a certain suspicion as insidious and even pernicious threats within the social order.

What the example from *The Secret Sharer* shows is that we need to think of cultural criticism as a verb—not as a noun that names positions but as a process—or as an odyssean journey of inquiring, teaching, and reading. Cultural criticism also needs to address the category of the aesthetic and its relationship to the political and the ethical. Now that literary studies have returned in the past decade to a criticism that focuses on contexts, we need to ask what is the place of the aesthetic in cultural criticism, why do we find some works beautiful, moving, and pleasing, and why do we respond to the quality and integrity of mimesis—the way the parts of a work are unified—as well as other formal ingredients of a work, including narrative voice, verbal texture, and characterization. How can we speak of ethical and political value without surrendering the value of the aesthetic? We do not have to subscribe to the view that an artwork is a self-contained ontology, its value intrinsic to itself, to ask how we can maintain a place for the aesthetic. Indeed, in his concept of catharsis, Aristotle focused on the role of the perceiver and insisted on the role of the structure of effects, on what the work does to the reader, as central to its aesthetic.

In my own work—mostly in the field of high modernism but also in the area of Holocaust narratives—I have been explicitly and implicitly proposing the ingredients of a humanistic cultural criticism that has a place for the aesthetic. It seeks to define cultural configurations that go beyond positivistic influence studies, and stresses recreating the economic, social, and political world authors inhabit. It tries to show an awareness of the cultural position of the critic and to understand interpretive history as a history of awareness—of aesthetic assumptions, political interests, and world views—but also as an idiosyncratic history of individual critics. While retaining a place for the aesthetic, humanistic criticism seeks a dialogue among various social, economic, and historical factors, between literature and history, between literature and the arts.

VII. The Power of Reading: Raising the Stakes

Anyone doubting the value of reading texts needs to read Azar Nafisi's *Reading 'Lolita' in Tehran: A Memoir* (2003), a text in which she foregrounds the human experience of the odyssey of reading. Nafisi speaks eloquently of the power of books to transform lives at a time in Tehran when many universities are closed and western canonical texts forbidden. What her book teaches us is that books have urgency and significance by raising crucial issues that touch on our very lives. She writes compellingly about defending *The Great Gatsby* at a mock trial after one of her male students complained that the novel was immoral because the characters are shallow and materialistic, a complaint raised because the student believed that "novels and their characters became our models in real life" (Nafisi 2003, 129). The mock trial becomes a teaching device to open the doors and windows of her students' minds to cultural differences and similarities.

Nafisi sees herself learning Gatsby's lesson:

> He wanted to fulfill his dream by repeating the past, and in the end he discovered that the past was dead, the present a sham, and there was no future. Was this not similar to our revolution, which had come in the name of our collective past and had wrecked our lives in the name of a dream? (Nafisi 2003, 144)

Gatsby's dream, like the revolution of the Ayatollahs, had become a consuming obsession; and like both Gatsby and the Ayatollahs, the purity of the dream makes it impossible to distinguish fantasy from reality.

Nafisi eloquently argues for what *The Great Gatsby* has in common with the other novels her group has been reading together:

> Imagination in these works is equated with empathy; we can't experience all that others have gone through, but we can understand even the more monstrous individuals in works of fiction. A good novel is one that shows the complexity of individuals, and creates enough space for all these characters to have a voice. [...] Empathy lies at the heart of [*The Great Gatsby*]; the biggest sin is to be blind to others' problems and pains. (Nafisi 2003, 131)

When the stakes are high, we tend to remember why *we do read*; indeed it is those occasions that bring a humanistic ethos to the fore.

Zarrin, one of Nafisi's students, understands that Tom, Daisy, and Jordan are "careless" people in that they lack the capacity to care about others, as opposed to Gatsby who cares too much, but only about one person and is careless about others. Careless of truth, Jordan compulsively lies and cheats. Indeed Nick's name "Carraway"— Care Away (that is, throw cares away or be oblivious to) or Carried Away (that is, to care too much as Nick does for Gatsby) reminds us of Nick's sometimes similarity to and sometimes difference from Gatsby.

What I like about Nafisi's text is that she shows her students—and us—what reading can mean. What she does is let them see into a world of personal relationships and their cost. While Gatsby's taking the blame for Daisy's running down Myrtle Wilson is his ultimate personal sacrifice, Nafisi's students have only been taught to measure sacrifice by such words as "masses," "revolution," and "Islam": "Passion and betrayal were for them political emotions and love an emotion supposed to be far removed from the stirrings of Jay Gatsby for Mrs. Tom Buchanan. Adultery in Tehran was one of so many other crimes, and the law dealt with it accordingly: public stoning" (108–9).

After reading Nafisi, I was and am affected by my reading in ways that transcend reading as an exercise or verbal game. Even now when I read Melville's "Benito Cerino," I am moved beyond measure by the incredible optimism and poignant blindness of Captain Amaso Delano who so desperately wants to see a harmonious universe and, like Gatsby, confuses dreams with reality.

Great texts can be read and reread many times over a lifetime, and each reading is a new odyssey of discovery. In a sense we are Gatsby always in our reading looking for the green light, the wonderful "orgiastic future that year by year recedes into the past." What I have learned is that we read to discover the absolutes that in our relative world—what Nick Carraway calls "the old unknown world"—only to discover with Nick and Gatsby that they are undiscoverable, and yet we continue our quest: "So we beat on, boats against the current, borne back ceaselessly in the past" (180). Nick—perhaps here something of a F. Scott Fitzgerald surrogate—recognizes the peculiar American innocence of this dream, the sense of "a fresh green breast of the new world" with infinite possibility, but sees that like all human possibility, it is something to be tainted by disappointment, incompleteness, and the shadow of mortality.

As readers we reach with Gatsby for a new world only to realize it must be, like our lives, caught in the sweep of human history and even more in the earth's history, "a transitory enchanted moment." For reading paradoxically enacts our mortality—books cease, narratives end, stories conclude—and we return to the tick tock of time, inevitably counting our life. But losing ourselves in the words and images of those dead and soon to be dead also affirms the immortality of the art and the human spirit. Thus William Shakespeare, Pablo Picasso, and Fitzgerald live and breathe in their creations, and for a moment we share their immortality.

VIII. Reading in Historical and Cultural Contexts

Cultural criticism has come to mean many things but it should include an awareness of similarities that go beyond the borderlines between art forms and between national literatures. Thus it is important to recognize that at the same time that Conrad, Joyce and Woolf were making experiments in writing fiction, Picasso and Georges Braque were embarking, in cubism, on similar experiments as painters. Writers and painters were scrambling the distinction between foreground and background, looking for new modes of representation, and including multiple perspectives on the same subject.

In a sense, color in painting provides the kind of energy and differentiation that Conrad's adjectives provide in his fiction. Thus a chapter of my *Rereading Conrad* entitled "The Influence of Gauguin on Conrad's *Heart of Darkness*" suggests how Paul Gauguin's Tahitian experience shaped Conrad's writing. I have suggested elsewhere that Gauguin, Picasso, and Henri Matisse, among others, were exploring man's primitive and atavistic antecedents during the approximate decade that Conrad was writing *Heart of Darkness* (1899), *Lord Jim* (1900), his other Malay novels (including *The Rescue*, which he did not publish until 1919), *Nostromo* (1904), and *The Secret Sharer* (1911).

Do we not need more discussion (and perhaps university courses) that juxtapose paintings such as Matisse's 1910 *Dance II* and its sequel *Music*—with their vermilion figures, blue sky, and green hill—not merely to major texts of British literature but to roughly contemporary texts of other literatures, such as Mann's *Death in Venice* (1912)? And, of course, we need discussions (and courses) that are attentive to parallel developments in music and dance and other art forms. But let me pursue the Matisse analogy for a moment.

Like figures in *Lord Jim*, Matisse's figures are poised between a realistic and an aesthetic world. *Dance II* enacts the primitive fantasy that informs Conrad's Congo and Patusan, including the female figures of the savage mistress and Jewel. In *Heart of Darkness* Marlow speaks about how he was tempted to go ashore for "a howl and a dance" with the savages. Matisse and Picasso—whose *Three Musicians* (1921) and *Three Dancers* (1925) are his comments on Matisse's *Dance II* and *Music*—would have endorsed Marlow's words in *Heart of Darkness*: "The mind of man is capable of anything—because everything is in it, all the past as well as the future." Modernism often includes a perspective and its own opposite or at least counterpart. Just as Matisse's reflective *Music* and libidinous and fantastic *Dance II* inform one another, so, too, in *Lord Jim* do Conrad's realist perspective of the *Patna* collision (and Jim's subsequent trial after the officers desert the ship) and Conrad's romance perspective of Patusan inform one another, and so in *Heart of Darkness* do Conrad's rendering of Kurtz's reversion to savagery and his rendering of Marlow's often reflective (and, later, retrospective) psychological responses.

IX. Stages in Our Odyssey of Reading

Some years ago I proposed a model of what happens when we read and I have tweaked it over the years. Even while acknowledging that my model is suggestive rather than rigorous, I believe that we do perceive in stages that move from a naive response or surface interpretation to critical or in-depth interpretation and, finally, to understanding our readings conceptually and ethically in terms of other knowledge.

Awareness of such stages enables us to understand our original odyssey of reading as well as an odyssey of understanding that begins during our actual reading and is continually modified by the subsequent linear (and chronological) process of reading the next words, pages, chapters, and books, and continues after reading. My stages are:

1.   *Immersion in the process of reading and the discovery of imagined worlds.* Reading is a place where text and reader meet in a transaction. As we open a text, we and the author meet as if together we were going to draw a map on an uncharted space. We partially suspend our sense of our world as we enter into the imagined world; we respond in experiential terms to the episodes, the story, the physical setting, the individualized characters as humans, and the telling voice. While it has become fashionable to speak dismissively of such reading as "naive," or the result of the "mimetic illusion," in fact how many of us do not read in that way with pleasure and delight—and with ethical judgments?

2.   *Quest for understanding.* Our quest for understanding is closely related to the diachronic, linear, temporal activity of reading. The quest speaks to the gap between "What did you say?" and "What did you mean?" In writing, as opposed to speech, the speaker cannot correct, intrude, or qualify; he cannot use gestures or adjust the delivery of his discourse. Because in writing we lack the speaker's help, we must make our own adjustments in our reading. As Paul Ricoeur notes, "What the text says now matters more than what the author meant to say, and every exegesis unfolds its procedures within the circumference of a meaning that has broken its moorings to the psychology of its author" (Ricoeur 1984, 191). In difficult and complex modern and postmodern texts, our search for necessary information may be much more of a factor than in traditional texts. In this stage, as we are actively unraveling the complexities of plot, we also seek to discover the principles or world view by which the author expects us to understand characters' behavior in terms of motives and values. Moreover, we make ethical judgments about intersubjective (read: personal) relations and authorial choices.

3.   *Self-conscious reflection.* Reflection speaks to the gap between "What did you mean?" and "What does that mean?" Upon reflection,

24

we may adjust our perspective or see new ones. What the interpretive reader does—particularly with spare, allusive (as well as elusive and illusive) modern literature—is to fill the gaps left by the text to create an explanatory text or Midrash on the text itself. As Wolfgang Iser puts it, "What is said only appears to take on significance as a reference to what is not said; it is the implications and not the statements that give shape and weight to the meaning" (quoted in Suleiman and Crossman 1980, 111). While the reader half-perceives, half-creates his original "immersed" reading of the text, he retrospectively—from the vantage point of knowing the whole—imposes shape and form on his story of reading. He discovers its significance in relation to his other experiences, including other reading experiences, and in terms of the interpretive communities to which he belongs. He reasons posteriorly from effects to causes. He is aware of referentiality to the anterior world—how that world informs the author's mimesis—and to the world in which he lives. He begins—more in modern texts, but even in traditional texts—to separate his own version of what is really meant from what is said, and to place ethical issues in the context of larger value issues.

Here Tzvetan Todorov's distinction between signification and symbolization is useful in defining how the reader moves from the imagined ontology to reflection: "Signified facts are understood: all we need is knowledge of the language in which the text is written. Symbolization facts are interpreted: and interpretations vary from one subject to another" (quoted in Suleiman and Crossman 1980, 73). A problem is that, in practice, what is understood or judged by one reader as signified facts may require interpretation or a different ethical judgment by another.

4. *Critical analysis.* As Paul Ricoeur writes, "To understand a text is to follow its movement from sense to reference, from what it says to what it talks about" (1984, 214). In the process, we always move from signifier to signified; for no sooner do we understand what the original signifiers signify within the imagined world than these signifieds in turn become signifiers for larger issues and symbolic constructions in the world beyond the text. We respond in terms of the values enacted by the text and, as with my example from Eliot's "Gerontion"—or, Pound's anti-Semitism—resist where texts disturb our sense of fairness.

While the reader responds to texts in such multiple ways and for such diverse reasons that we cannot speak of a correct reading, we can speak of a dialogue among plausible readings. Drawing upon our interpretive strategies, we reflect on generic, intertextual, linguistic, and biographical relationships that disrupt linear reading; we move back and forth from the whole to the part. As Ricoeur writes: "The reconstruction of the text as a whole is implied in the recognition of the parts. And reciprocally, it is in constructing the details that we construe the whole" (1984, 204). My responses to my reading are a function of what I know, what I have recently been reading, my last experience of reading a particular author, my knowledge of the period in which the author wrote as well as the influences upon him or his influence on others, and my current values. My responses also depend both on how willing I am to suspend my sense of irony and detachment and enter into the imagined world of the text and on how much of the text my memory retains.

5. *Cognition in terms of what we know.* In a continuation of our fourth stage, we return to the original reading experience of the text and subsequently modify our conceptual hypotheses about the genre, period, author, canon, themes, and most of all, values. We also integrate what we have read into our reading of other texts and into our way of looking at ourselves and the world. Here we consciously use our values and our categorizing sensibility—our rage for order—to make sense of our reading experience and our way of being in our world. In the final stage, the interpretive reader may become a critic who writes his own text about the "transaction" between himself and the text—and this response has an ethical component.

X. Interpretive Communities

Just as an author "rents" multiple linguistic systems to create what Mikhail Bakhtin calls heteroglossia, the reader "rents" diverse interpretive strategies—or perspectives—depending upon his prior experience. But we each belong to multiple interpretive communities, and as we read, we draw upon our participation and experience in several interpretive communities. Not only do those interpretive communities change as well as modify and subvert one another, but also our relationship to them varies from text to text. How we read the texts—and the world—depends on an ever-changing hierarchy of interpretive strategies. These hierarchies constitute our reading of texts—and the world—even as they are constituted by it. That is, as we read, our interpretive strategies are challenged and modified even as they modify what we read. When reading criticism we need to be aware of the theoretical and methodological assumptions that produce a reading and examine whether we belong to the community of readers who share those assumptions.

We need to account for the subjectivity inherent in our reading. For may not subjectivity idiosyncratically deflect us from the decision about which interpretive communities we shall use? We also need be self-conscious about the distinctiveness of our position in relation to the text that we are describing or responding to. If someone were to read my interpretive criticism or come to my classes, he would be aware of my propensity for seeing texts in historical, mimetic, and formal terms—especially my propensity as a pragmatic Aristotelian to hear the voice of narrators and to stress the relationship between Doesness and Isness. And what about my personal background and experience? My biases and shortcomings? Do I not have a greater professional and personal stake in some texts than in others?

What I am suggesting is that the reader as *übermensch* or as super-reader is a disguise for the human reader with all his tics and quirks. Thus, if we wish to enter into a dialogue with other approaches, we need to understand the deflection caused by our subjectivity and that of the interpretive critics we read. It may be worth the effort to induce from each interpretive text a persona of the critic to see if we can explain his subjectivity and thus understand his underlying perspective, approach, values, methods, and theory. That is, we must read critical texts as if they too were spoken by a human voice to a human audience, and—as if we were hearing a first-person narration—we must attend to what is missing or distorted.

27

Finally, the largest number of members in any interpretive community of readers is one. All criticism is disguised autobiography. We take our own journeys of reading and they are not quite the same as the journeys of others; nor are they the same when we reread.

XI. Launching an Odyssey of Reading: Notes on an Embarkation

Originally educated as a formalist, reasonably early in my career I began to live by the mantra, "Always the text; always historicize." What follows is the way such an odyssey of reading might be launched with reference to Conrad's *The Secret Agent* (1907). I am struck by the way that so many of Conrad's novels take us from the opening sentence into a unique imagined world. Upon rereading, we see how the opening paragraphs establish a grammar of psychological, political, and moral cause and effect. For example, let us turn to *The Secret Agent*:

> Mr. Verloc, going out in the morning, left his shop nominally in charge of his brother-in-law. It could be done, because there was very little business at any time, and practically none at all before evening. Mr. Verloc cared but little about his ostensible business. And, moreover, his wife was in charge of his brother-in-law.

The disjunction between behavior and motive which is at the center of private and political life in Conrad's turn-of-the-century London is foreshadowed in this opening paragraph. Verloc's real business is spying, although the soft porn he peddles in his shop serves as a cover for his illicit relationship with Vladimir and the British Police. Pretending to be an anarchist, he is actually in the pay of the embassy of an unnamed authoritarian country. We learn that everyone is in charge, or thinks he is, of others but those at the top often have their own secret plans. "Ostensible" business is a disguise for a more complex group of motives. Written large in the above passages are essential Conradian themes: 1) the discrepancy between, on the one hand, dimly acknowledged needs, obsessions, and compulsions and, on the other, actual behavior; 2) the distinction between actual behavior and articulated motive—that is, the story we tell ourselves about ourselves.

I want to show how this embarkation looks from the perspective of the completed journey. Conrad's conservative desire for a few simple moral and political ideas is at odds with his often-remarked skepticism. Yet he is not a cynic or a nihilist; he believes that within a morally neutral universe, humans can create islands of tentative meaning, even if from an objective perspective those islands are illusions. *The Secret Agent*'s meaning depends on a self-dramatizing narrator willfully separating himself from a world he despises, only to gradually emerge in his telling as a character with his own humanistic values. Choreographing cynicism, Conrad creates a narrator whose cold, detached style aggressively reduces the characters to formal elements; the narrator is always evaluating, controlling, and restraining the nihilism of the world he describes with such disdain.

That an important pleasure of reading derives from our understanding a text's unity and how the parts relate to the whole is particularly true for Conrad's texts. The consonance between Conrad's beginnings and endings are remarkable and one of the reason his works are so satisfying. Every aspect functions in terms of an aesthetic whole. As *The Secret Agent* concludes with the psychotic figure known as the Professor, we think not only of Stevie's—Verloc's brother-in-law's—last fatal walk in Greenwich but also of Verloc's walk to the Embassy of an unnamed totalitarian regime where he is intimidated—indeed terrorized—by Vladimir, the regime's political operative in England, into planning the bombing, which will supposedly arouse a desire for repression:

> And the incorruptible Professor walked, too, averting his eyes from the odious multitude of mankind. He had no future. He disdained it. He was a force. His thoughts caressed the images of ruin and destruction. He walked, frail, insignificant, shabby, miserable—and terrible in the simplicity of his idea calling madness and despair to the regeneration of the world. Nobody looked at him. He passed on unsuspected and deadly, like a pest in the street full of men.

29

Does not the psychotic, narcissistic Professor—a human perambulatory explosive device—make us aware of the ironic disjunction between those espousing radical politics and the human life they supposedly wish to improve? Does not his cynicism recall that of the debonair Vladimir who also revels in images of mindless violence even while being treasured as a social pet by British high society? The Professor emphasizes the nocturnal and self-serving activities of society's protectors, Inspector Heat and the Assistant Commissioner, who themselves mysteriously walk about London driven by their own private motives. Their behavior recalls the tolerance of Nazi sympathizers by the British in the 1930s, which Kazuo Ishiguro has highlighted in his *The Remains of the Day*, a novel with Conradian resonance.

Fueled by New Historicism, current odysseys of reading put great stress on historical context, sometimes to the detriment of close reading. In keeping with the renewed emphasis on historical context, much has been made of the source material for Conrad's anarchists in *The Secret Agent*. The novel's central anarchic incident is based upon the Greenwich Bomb Outrage of 1894 when a man named Martial Bourdin had, like Stevie, killed himself setting off a bomb in Greenwich Park near the Royal Observatory. Bourdin's brother-in-law, H.B. Samuels, like Verloc, was a police agent. But whether detailed knowledge of source material is essential to understanding how Conrad imaginatively transmuted factual material is moot. Rather, Conrad's characterizations in *The Secret Agent* depend on his discovering apt tropes for recognizable political types of the right and left, types which barely need contextual explanation. Put another way, "Always historicize" means examining how historical contexts inform and enrich a text rather than following endless tangents that take readers into byways and tributaries.

When we read of the terrorists in *The Secret Agent*, we recognize in them today's psychotic racists, violent anti-abortionists, plane hijackers, and political terrorists seeking to destroy regimes they dislike, as well as the right-wing fanatics who bombed a federal building in Oklahoma City. Listen to Yundt, one of the anarchists in *The Secret Agent*: "No pity for anything on earth, including themselves, and death enlisted for good and ill in the service of humanity—that's what

I would have liked to see" (*The Secret Agent*, 47). The professor dreams of delivering a violent "startling" "blow fit to open the first crack in the imposing edifice of legal conceptions sheltering the atrocious injustice of society" (*The Secret Agent*, 76).

XII. Returning Home: An Example of Disembarkation

If each beginning is a genesis, each ending is an apocalypse reordering what has preceded. But let us use our metaphor of the odyssey and think about the close of a particular striking odyssey of reading in another frequently taught text.

Gabriel's transformation at the end of Joyce's *The Dead* is for him a personal one—one that does not free the rest of the Dublin residents from moral and spiritual paralysis but is a moment of hope rendered as a performance in which the reader participates:

> Generous tears filled Gabriel's eyes. He had never felt like that himself towards any woman but he knew that such a feeling must be love. The tears gathered more thickly in his eyes and in the partial darkness he imagined he saw the form of a young man standing under a dripping tree. Other forms were near. His soul had approached that region where dwell the vast hosts of the dead. He was conscious of, but could not apprehend, their wayward and flickering existence. His own identity was fading out into a grey impalpable world; the solid world itself that these dead had one time reared and lived in was dissolving and dwindling.
>
> A few light taps upon the pane made him turn to the window. It had begun to snow again. He watched sleepily the flakes, silver and dark, falling obliquely against the lamplight. The time had come for him to set out on his journey westward. Yes, the newspapers were right; snow was general all over Ireland. It was falling on every part of the dark central plain, on the treeless hills, falling softly upon the Bog of Allen and, farther westward, softly falling into the dark mutinous Shannon waves. It was falling, too, upon every part of the lonely churchyard on the hill where Michael Furey lay buried. It lay thickly drifted on the crooked crosses and headstones, on the spears of the

31

little gate, on the barren thorns. His soul swooned slowly as he heard the snow falling faintly through the universe and faintly falling, like the descent of their last end, upon all the living and the dead. (The Dead, 59)

What is performed is the suspension of rational and linear thought. While, as we know from John Huston's wonderful film *The Dead*, the passage can be visualized, does it not enact a state of being that finally transcends the visual, a state when the soul, as W.B. Yeats puts it in "Sailing to Byzantium," "clap[s] its hands and sing[s]." For loving Gretta, for understanding that passion is itself a value, Gabriel is rewarded with serenity, an escape from his concerns, and an understanding that passion is a value: "Better pass boldly into that other world, in the full glory of some passion, than fade and wither dismally with age." We may recall that in *Ulysses* the vision of Rudy is Bloom's reward for taking care of Stephen in Dublin's night town.

Discursively, the last sentence makes little sense. One cannot hear snow falling through the universe and the antecedent of "their" is indeterminate (snowflakes? all the dead? Gretta and Michael? Gretta, Michael, and himself? all the past and future dead?). Gabriel's move outside the enclosure of his ego is enabled/performed by the phonics and reversals of the passage, particularly the last sentence. The passage's meaning derives from its place in a process; it contrasts with the mimesis of the preceding pages of the story and with Gabriel's paralytic self-consciousness, rationality, and literalism.

The ending is discourse not story; yet as discourse it shows us what Gabriel needs but lacks: song, lyricism, metaphoricity, escape from time into non-rational, passionate states of being, a loosening of the bonds of self-consciousness. The dissolution of Gabriel's ego is for him a positive move because he can surrender to the lyrical moment, to a time when the soul claps hands and sings. In a sense, at this moment he joins the dance of life, or thinks he does. It is a moment of rare serenity—visual, tonal, emotional serenity—a moment which resists (perhaps resents?) the critic's rational efforts to order it because it is allegorical and asyntactical. Even while acknowledging the brilliance of John Huston's visualization, do we not feel that it encroaches on our interior experience, on our private admiration of the scene and reduces our rich, poly-auditory response to Gabriel's interior life and Joyce's rendering of it to a sequence of visual images? Isn't that often the problem when we see our intimate reading experience transformed into a film?

What is absent is as important as what is present in responding to character. The snow imagery focuses our attention on a world outside Gabriel—a natural world where generations live and die, thus rendering an individual's sense of self-importance irrelevant. We recall that snow has the potential to become ice (death) and water (life). Obviously, as ice it also suggests the emotional sterility of a world reduced to social gestures, empty talk, and loveless relationships— a world where a tiny pathetic "I" cannot connect to others to form a loving, passionate, tender couple, a world that does not even give Gabriel the feeling he so desperately needs—namely that of being part of a social mosaic. We can never be sure whether Gretta is waiting for Gabriel in the way that Molly is waiting for Bloom, because we see less of Gabriel's dignity and integrity than we see of Bloom's and more of Gabriel's selfishness and narrow-mindedness. Perhaps we do not quite sympathize with Gabriel's sense of isolation and disappointment as we do with Bloom's because of the latter's generous concern for others—such as Paddy Dignam's family and Mrs. Purefoy.

Note how fiction's realistic code reasserts itself when basic emotions of love and death are the subject. We respond powerfully to descriptions of Gabriel's transformation and use psychological grammar to understand that transformation, including his realization that conscience and self-consciousness are not the full parameters of living, that the love shared by Michael and Gretta contained passion, intensity, and intimacy that go beyond concern with whether or not Gretta wears galoshes. We might therefore speak of the precedence of subjects and note how our aesthetic sense itself is more likely to be pushed aside and relegated to the back burner when we are engaged by issues that matter to our human feelings—notably, issues of the human psyche. And we might say that most of us will be engaged mainly by the representation of emotions that interest us. Indeed, in speaking of the precedence and hierarchy of subjects that engage us, should we not acknowledge that a culture's ever-changing preferences, together with its continuing interest in certain themes and problems such as adult sexual love, help create and recreate its literary canon?

XIII. Conclusion: Professing Reading within the University and Beyond

As humanists, we need to look beyond the academy and take part in larger discussions about what we read and how and why we read. We need to be stakeholders in public discussions of the role of the humanities and to argue for the role of imaginative literature in opening the doors and windows of our minds. We need to articulate why the study of literature matters. We need to clearly and precisely explain why we do what we do and why it matters, and be willing to engage audiences beyond those specialists who do what we do. We need to develop a rhetoric of engagement and to acknowledge that the discussion of values—how they are shaped by history and how by individual obsessions, compulsions, and dimly acknowledged needs—is not only literature's subject but also the reason many of us read. We need articulate the joy we experience in seeing how Thackeray, Conrad, Joyce, Woolf, and George Eliot bend language to meet their artistic goals, and we need explain how their stylistic experimentations are necessary and sufficient for their meaning. When we as literature professors do our research on literary texts, we need not be overly modest about making claims for the production of knowledge even while understanding that there are other critical constructs with other definitions of knowledge.

Even while rejoicing in Joyce and the other wonderful texts I have been discussing, I want to discuss, too, an issue that should concern us academics, namely the danger of insularity—the danger that we burrow deeply into our areas of interest without communicating to the body of readers who want us to present our insights and discoveries not in academic jargon but in language that they understand. We need to tell our stories of reading in ways that appeal to a wider audience and share with them the passion we feel for our subject and the reasons we feel that passion and joy. We do an injustice to our study of literature if we fail to build a bridge between our scholarship and the larger audience of non-academics who read with pleasure. When we write as teachers we should not simply write as if we were in the eighth week of a graduate seminar or a colloquium. Rather, we must as scholars and teachers articulate what we do not only for specialists but for students we are mentoring, undergraduates who come for the first time to the texts we love—whether it be Shakespeare, Woolf or Toni Morrison—and readers in the world beyond the academy who turn to us for our ability to open the doors and windows of complex texts. We need to remember, too, that our students live in the world beyond the classroom, and we need teach them to speak articulately, read perspicaciously, and think critically. What we do as teachers is not merely convey knowledge but grow young adults.

In the age of the Internet where reading often means taking in brief messages and communication depends on cell phones, text-messaging, and email, we need to make a case not only for reading books, but for reading difficult and time-consuming books. In this vein, I would like to briefly return to a fundamental question "Why do we read?" I know it is hard to separate our roles as literary intellectuals and scholars making our careers from this fundamental question, but it is an urgent question. Don't we read to complement our own experience of life? To learn how others make sense of human life? To journey elsewhere into different places and back-wards (and sometimes forwards) in time? To see complex ethical dilemmas dramatized within a narrative structure and to watch imag-ined characters sort through them? In our reading we make judg-ments and evaluations, even while we learn to be sympathetic and empathetic.

Nor should we forget that we read for pleasure—the local delights of seeing how language can be shaped to do wonders and the larger delights of the wonders of life and the understanding of what humans live—and, on occasion—die for. We should not be embarrassed to see characters within imagined ontologies as representations of how humans live and, indeed, we can learn much from watching the results of Kurtz's moral absolutism and pathological reversion to savagery, from the Captain's commitment to his task in *The Secret Sharer*, and from Leopold Bloom's resilience, curiosity, and reliance on his core values of decency and generosity.

We must, I repeat, never forget that books are by humans, about humans, and for humans. We need to pay attention to what is represented in texts and what we learn from the dramatizations of human behavior within texts, all the while realizing these representations and dramatizations are the result of skillful artistry and are metaphors for real people.

While I was thinking about a keynote address I was to give at a Joyce conference in 2005, my mother died little more than a year after my father's death. Her final illness was quite awful and so was my father's the year before. Not surprisingly I was tempted to descend into my personal Hades as I thought about the ephemeral nature of life, my place now as the oldest survivor in my immediate family, and the horrors of growing old. I found some solace in the way Joyce's Bloom overcomes his own disappointments by affirming life: "Plenty to see and hear and feel yet. Feel live warm beings near you. Let them sleep in their maggoty beds. They are not going to get me this innings. Warm beds: warm fullblooded life."

I should like to close this chapter with the Constantine Cavafy poem entitled "Ithaka." Cavafy's poem speaks not only to life as an odyssey but also to the odyssey of reading. It suggests Ithaca as a metaphor for the completion of a text and for the correlation between our reading texts and our understanding—to cite Stevens in "The Idea of Order at Key West"—"of ourselves and of our origins."

Ithaka

As you set out for Ithaka
hope your road is a long one,
full of adventure, full of discovery, Laistrygonians, Cyclops,
angry Poseidon—don't be afraid of them:
you'll never find things like that on your way
as long as you keep your thoughts raised high,
as long as a rare excitement

stirs your spirit and your body.
Laistrygonians, Cyclops,
wild Poseidon—you won't encounter them
unless you bring them along inside your soul,
unless your soul sets them up in front of you.

Hope your road is a long one.
May there be many summer mornings when
with what pleasure, what joy,
you enter harbours you're seeing for the first time;
may you stop at Phoenician trading stations
to buy fine things,
mother of pearl and coral, amber and ebony,
sensual perfume of every kind—
as many sensual perfumes as you can;
and may you visit many Egyptian cities
to learn and go on learning from their scholars.

Keep Ithaka always in your mind.
Arriving there is what you're destined for.
But don't hurry the journey at all.
Better if it lasts for years,
so you're old by the time you reach the island,
wealthy with all you've gained on the way,
not expecting Ithaka to make you rich.

Ithaka gave you the marvelous journey.
Without her you wouldn't have set out.
She has nothing left to give you now.

And if you find her poor, Ithaka won't have fooled you.
Wise as you will have become, so full of experience,
you'll have understood by then what these Ithakas mean.

Is not the goal of each of our odysseys of reading to have a "marvelous journey [...] so full of experiences?"

2

How We Learn and What We Learn from Literary Texts

I. Introduction

It is somewhat old-fashioned to claim that we understand life better by reading imaginative literature. Yet I contend that we do. Non-fiction helps us know; imaginative literature—fiction, poetry, and drama—helps us understand both ourselves and the world beyond ourselves. To say this is to agree with Matthew Arnold that literature presents a criticism of life, but it is also to go much further by arguing that reading literature is a crucial part of life along with experiencing the visual arts, music, architecture, drama, and film.

There are many ways this happens: 1) we identify with the narrative voice or we distance ourselves from that voice, be it a first-person speaker or an omniscient narrator; 2) in much the same way, we identify with or distance characters; 3) reading imaginative literature enhances our life experience by taking us into imagined worlds; 4) reading imagined work increases our political and moral awareness; 5) imagined works complement and often deepen our historical knowledge; paradoxically, this may happen even when the facts are not exactly accurate if the text speaks to the warp and woof of lived life at a particular time; 6) imaginative literature is an important part of the history of ideas and enacts important philosophical visions; 7) we learn about authors' psyches and values and the way they saw the world and why; and 8) imaginative literature increases the pleasures of our travels and vice versa.

Narratives teach. Let me make clear the assumptions about narrative that underlie my thinking. Narrative organizes experience into a necessary, probable, and meaningful plot about human actions; we respond to plot as a process, as a structure of affects, that continually proposes, qualifies, undermines, questions, and reformulates patterns of meaning—patterns which are, of course, conveyed by language but which move beyond discrete words to form mimetic units.

Narrative is both the representation of external events and the telling of those events. My interest in narrative derives from my belief that we make sense of our life by ordering it and giving it shape. The stories we tell ourselves provide continuity among the concatenation of diverse episodes in our lives, even if our stories inevitably distort and falsify. Each of us is continually writing and rewriting the text of our lives, revising our memories and hopes, proposing plans, filtering disappointments through our defenses and rationalizations, and making adjustments in the way we present ourselves to ourselves and others. To the degree that we are self-conscious, we live in our narratives—our discourse—about our actions, thoughts, and feelings. While there is always a gulf between imagined worlds and real ones, does not the continuity between reading lives and reading texts depend on understanding reading as a means of sharpening our perceptions, cultivating discriminations, and deepening our insights about ourselves? For reading is a process of cognition that depends on actively organizing the phenomena of language both in the moment of perception and in the fuller under-standing that develops as our reading continues as well as in our retrospective view of our completed reading.

When reading as well as teaching a text, we need to situate it in the political and historical context; we need situate a text within the author's life and values and the time in which he wrote; and we need explore first and foremost the values he enacts. By examining in some detail a handful of diverse imaginative texts written within the last century or so, I want to think about how books teach us how to read them and how their significant form embodies meaning that is urgent and important.

II. Joyce's *Dubliners*: What We Learn from Joyce

While writing *Dubliners*, Joyce had many audiences in mind: Dublin's drowsing citizens whose consciences and consciousness needed arousing; the Catholic hierarchy; the Irish artistic and intellectual elite, including Yeats; the British public; readers of English and those who read in translation and perhaps a prospective publisher for his collection of stories. In 1904 Joyce published early versions of several stories in *Dubliners* ("The Sisters," "Eveline," and "After the Race"); the novella *The Dead*, the final piece to be written, was completed in 1907. In the first three stories—"The Sisters," "An Encounter," and "Araby"— Joyce uses a young boy to demonstrate the values of a representative preadolescent in Dublin and to show the way that Catholicism and British domination of Ireland shape the boy's epistemology and language, even as the speaker performs for us the consequences of that upbringing.

Joyce resented deeply that England had let a patronizing Anglo-Irish Protestant oligarchy dominate Ireland, and knew that colonial powers—whatever their stated intention about bringing progress and enlightenment to the colonized people—dedicated their energies to maintaining power. That Ireland's population had been halved by famine in the nineteenth century aroused the anger of the Irish public, including Irish writers such as Joyce; they held England responsible for milking Irish resources and ignoring Irish problems. Joyce knew, too, how the Irish sought refuge from imperialism in the Catholic Church. As Mary Gordon writes:

> But if the relationship with Mother England was fragile and vexed [...] there was the Rock of Peter upon which the church stood [... W]hatever the winds blowing across the Irish Sea, the breath of the Holy Spirit could be felt every time a nun or a priest opened his or her mouth. (2003)

The Irish reader, too, is a particular audience that Joyce had in mind; he sees that the Irish lapsed soul must be restored and each Irish person must rediscover his humanity so that Dublin can become healthy and whole. Joyce wants to teach imperfect Irish readers to make sense of Dublin by showing them what Dublin really is. What Giuseppe Mazzotta has written about in Dante's *Divine Comedy* is just as true of *Dubliners*: it "dramatizes in a fundamental way the activity of interpretation—it recounts the effort of the poet-exegete to read the book of the world" (Reynolds 1981, 220). Joyce is reading the book of Dublin for us. Like Dante, we are pilgrim-spectators, and Joyce is Virgil showing us the inferno of contemporary Dublin. The reader, accompanied by the narrator-guide, sees the landscape of Dublin and is urged to think of the possibility for renewal. The reader in his sense-making must establish not only hierarchies among his critical approaches, but also hierarchies among the details. Our reading iterates the characters' efforts to make sense of the world, but our reading must go beyond their sense-making. *Dubliners* teaches the reader that he must abandon Dublin-think and Dublin-speak if he is to find meaning. Because the reader's sense-making involves fulfilled expectations and understood patterns, his activity is at odds with the frustrated quests of most of the figures in *Dubliners*. But because in "Araby" the speaker's telling reveals that he is only at a resting place and that he has the resources of language and imagination to resume the struggle to discover meaning in his quest, the reader may have more in common with the speaker in "Araby" than with the other protagonists and narrators.

In *Dubliners* we see the totality of Dublin life and the evolving patterns that hold Joyce's visions of the city together even when aspects of that pattern are located in different stories. We see stories in a spatial configuration as if they were stars in a constellation held together by what might be called the magnetism of significance. We should think of *Dubliners* as an evolving series of stories, a kaleidoscope in which each story takes a turn as the centerpiece in the pattern. The episodes cohere into what may be called a mindscape of Dublin and enact the repetitious cycle of blunted aspiration and frustration, of crass materialism, of sexual repression, of drunkenness, of moral idiocy. *Dubliners* is a cityscape, a representation of Dublin; as such it looks forward to, and becomes part of, Joyce's later depictions of Dublin's characters in *Ulysses* and *Finnegans Wake*.

Joyce's work teaches us a great deal about Ireland. His texts are set in Ireland before Ireland became an independent country. With irony and cynicism, he writes about the effects of British rule and Catholicism's presence. In "Araby," he teaches us about the effects on a boy at the edge of puberty of being taught that sex is sinful and that his business is to obey his clerical masters. He also teaches that within a colonial atmosphere even dreams are polluted by colonialism; when the boy takes his magical mystery tour to a fair called "Araby," he finds that even the promise of excitement is ruined by indifferent British who are flirting with one another. Nor does Joyce spare the Irish for their paralyses: verbosity, sloth, alcoholism, and nostalgia for the past distract the Irish from getting hold of their own lives.

In *Ulysses*, Joyce shows how the Irish require a mature artist who will eschew calls for violence or escape into a mystical vision and provide an anatomy of what Ireland and especially Dublin needs. By writing the epic of Irish life in 1904, he teaches his reader the necessity of such human values as family love, dignity, courage, and integrity, and he does so by dramatizing how an Irish Jew lives with anti-Semitism and hostility. He affirms, too, by his dramatization of the relationship between Molly and Bloom, the importance of both romantic and sexual love as touchstones of human existence.

III. Learning from Conrad's Political Vision

Why, no matter what the critical fashion, has Conrad spoken to readers for a century? If it is in large part his psychological subtlety and political complexity, it is also because we recognize on every page parallels to both our private lives and public reality. We recognize our reality in his ironic skepticism of all dogma. Conrad always writes as the outsider, the marginalized figure who does not quite belong. For example, in *Under Western Eyes* (1911) he sees the peculiar parallel between the solitary and lonely betrayer, Razumov, and the fastidious western language teacher and narrator. With a perspective that anticipates contemporary views of cultural production, he also understands the difference between the rationality and morality of western democracy and the fanaticism and cynicism produced by Russian autocracy. He understands how politics is a mosaic of individual motives.

New Historicism and its offspring, postcolonial studies, have brought renewed interest to Conrad's political vision. *Heart of Darkness* (1899) is a visionary text that exposed King Leopold II of Belgium's rapacious exploitation of the Congo and, by implication, colonial imperialism. While the megalomaniacal Leopold ruled the Congo Free State from 1885 to 1908, the native population was cut in half by his predatory practices. His regime ravaged the land, destroyed the food supplies with resulting famine, forced people to labor in terrible conditions with little or no pay, and demanded unreasonable production quotas of rubber and ivory. To break the will of the natives, Leopold's army and minions either took their native colonial subjects hostage or tortured and killed them. The Europeans also introduced new diseases into the Congolese population.

Thus, in *Heart of Darkness*, we need ask, what attitudes do imperialists take to the natives and why? Is it, as Marxists would contend, a story about the "commodity fetishism" of later capitalism? Is it, as Chinua Achebe has claimed, a racist drama whose images reinforce white stereotypes about the dichotomy of black and white? Is *Heart of Darkness* an imperialistic romance about the conquest of Africa? Or is it more accurate to stress how it is an ironic inversion, a bathetic reification, of such a genre? Are black and white and light and dark always equated with the polarity of civilization and savagery, good and evil, corrupt and innocent, or is the dialectic of images subtler than that?

Conrad plays on the clichés and shibboleths of his era, when Africa was the "dark continent"—the place of mystery and secrets—and the primitive continent where passions and emotions dominated reason and intellect. He asks us to consider whether we can cross cultural boundaries without transgressing them. Perhaps we then need to ask: in situating himself as a critical and ironic respondent to imperialistic exploitation, is Marlow able to separate himself from colonial domination? And can we as white Europeans and Americans teach a story like *Heart of Darkness* in a western classroom without reinscribing ourselves as colonialists? When we teach *Heart of Darkness*, are we in the same position as western museums displaying non-western art with little understanding of its context; that is, are we invading a different culture with our texts about colonialism? Whether in Ireland, Malaysia, or Africa, western colonialism for the most part despoiled the people and the land it touched.

But let us remember that *Heart of Darkness* speaks with passion about the issues of colonialism and empire. If we can understand the agon as an enactment of how the natives' energy and instincts have been corrupted by materialistic, overly rational imperialists, we can see that the charge of racism is itself reductive.

Heart of Darkness debunks the concept of the white man's burden and shows how the concept of empire is a sham. Conrad chooses to show Kurtz's "Exterminate the Brutes" as a stunning abandonment of the moral pretensions on which imperialism is based. Kurtz's radical transformation exposes his own reductive perspective and that of Marlow, King Leopold of Belgium, other Europeans—indeed, all of us who would seek to adopt a position whereby one culture views another from a stance of superiority. For his era Conrad was avant-garde in acknowledging that at times Africans were more controlled and ethically advanced than westerners; he, like Gauguin, knew that native cultural practices and their art—chants, dance, drumming— were alien to western concepts of display, that their art was religious in function, linking daily experience to abstract beliefs, and that their art was used performatively in funerals, weddings, and initiation rites.

We learn from Marlow's tale and the frame narrator how we each necessarily make our own meaning. Conrad recognizes the distinction between how events occur and how we remember them, and between how we remember them and the verbal constructions we discover to tell them. He realizes our versions of events, like the versions of Marlow, the captain-narrator in *The Secret Sharer* (1910), and Jim in *Lord Jim* (1900) are self-created constructions, which fulfill their tellers psychic and moral needs. Put another way, to quote Marlow in *Heart of Darkness*, "we live, as we dream—alone."

Marlow's decision to narrate his experience is predicated upon at least a tentative faith that language is the vehicle of order, reason, and symbolic light, and can serve as his intellectual guide to explore the mystery and darkness of the human soul. Marlow's tale deeply affects the nameless listener who becomes our narrator: "I raised my head. The offing was barred by a black bank of clouds, and the tranquil waterway leading to the uttermost ends of the earth flowed somber under an overcast sky—seemed to lead into the heart of an immense darkness" (162, the Kent edition [Garden City, NY: Doubleday, 1926]). Since the nameless narrator recreates his original process of learning the tale, we can assume that his comment about Marlow's inconclusive tales occurs before he has heard Marlow's tale and parallels Marlow's ingenuous assertion that he was like "a silly little bird" (52). The tale shatters the first speaker's innocence, which we have seen in his evocation of the greatness of England's epic past. As he listens, he becomes as fascinated with Marlow's voice as Marlow had been with Kurtz's voice, and turns to Marlow as if he were oracular:

> The others might have been asleep, but I was awake. I listened, I listened on the watch for the sentence, for the word, that would give me a clue to the faint uneasiness inspired by this narrative that seemed to shape itself without human lips in the heavy night-air of the river. (83)

The adaptation of Marlow's brooding tone and style of expression indicates that Marlow had communicated something of his experience. That Marlow communicates demonstrates that man does not live completely alone as he had claimed, and implies that language can establish the "fellowship" and "solidarity" that both Marlow and his creator seek.

Conrad's *Nostromo* (1904) is a prescient examination of how political zealotry is often disguised self-interest. Conrad's conservative desire for a few simple moral and political ideas is at odds with his oft-remarked skepticism. Conrad dramatizes how in the name of social ideals, violence, and destruction are unleashed within an imaginary South American country and that there is always—no matter what politics are subscribed to—a disjunction between individuals trying to affect history and the actual events.

Yet Conrad is not a cynic or a nihilist; he believes that within a morally neutral universe, humans can create islands of tentative meaning, even if from an objective perspective those islands are illusions. Conrad understands the necessity for political and social organization. While he dissects flaws in various systems, states, and communities, he does not propose alternative programs. But he does insist on preserving the freedom of the individual to live his own life as long as he does not pose a physical threat to others. What totalitarianism encourages is failure of responsibility, shallowness, thoughtlessness, and remoteness from personal ties and commitments to others.

Nostromo examines both natives and westerners as they fight for control of a prosperous area of Costaguano—an imagined country in South America with an uncanny resemblance to several twentieth-century Third World countries. He shows how the greed of Holroyd, the fanaticism of Father Corbelan, and the obsessiveness of Gould are complicit with the political machinations of those cynically seeking power for its own sake, often in the name of an abstraction that is a disguise for their own selfish motives.

Rereading *Nostromo* we see how each person projects his or her own expectations and desires upon the Italian chief of the *cargadores* who has been given by others the title that translates as "our man," although Nostromo is virtually anonymous and the novel offers only the vaguest hints of his personal past or national identity. Doesn't the way each character imputes value to Nostromo based on his or her self-interest—that is, in a way which fulfills his or her psychic needs, material desires, and political aspirations—anticipate the way we attribute values to sports heroes, actors, rock stars, and even political figures about whom we know little? Moreover, do not we see in the disjunction between the Goulds' public stature and their dysfunctional private life—Charles Gould obsessed with wrenching silver from the mines, his wife caught in the sterile formalism of a marriage gone awry—a foreshadowing of the marriages of more recent public figures?

Conrad never allows his reader to find a comfortable position; by testing a wide variety of attitudes in his fiction, he demands that his reader do the same. Just as his narrators and characters struggle to come to terms with experience, so must his readers. While we cannot be sure that Conrad is devoid of racial prejudice, *The Nigger of the*

"Narcissus" (1897) tests us as moral human beings because it shows that the protagonist, James Wait, is both an invalid and malingerer as well as the victim of stereotypical racist views.

As long as we are interested in political, community, and personal ethics and the complex psychological reasons we behave as we do, we can be assured of Conrad's prominence.

IV. *A Passage to India* as a Window on India

E.M. Forster's *A Passage to India* (1924) depends upon the ever-shifting relations among Hindus, Muslims, and English Christians. Our reading helps us understand the schismatic politics that later led to the separation of India into Pakistan and, later, Bangladesh. Certainly, the colonial system contributed to caste divisions. The caste system regulates many aspects of Hindu behavior. In 1947 India legally—but not quite effectively as yet—abolished the caste system and the category of untouchables. But in 1924, the year of *A Passage to India*, the caste system played an even larger role than it does today.

Forster understood that, whatever the original articulated ideals of the British in India—such as improving the economic lot of the backward colonized nation by introducing commerce, even as Britain administered justice and introduced a better education system—the purposes of the British empire had become (as is always the case with imperialism) the preservation of power. *A Passage to India* is based in part on Forster's desire to show that it is no longer possible—and certainly not possible in writing about a land suffering from British conquest—to write a Jane Austen-like novel without sacrificing artistic integrity. What do English ideas of personal relationships have to do with Godbole, the Hindu Brahmin, or the non-verbal, handsome untouchable who turns the fan at Aziz's trial? For where there is empire, the tradition of manners becomes so skewed—we recall the bathetic bridge party at the English club in chapter 5—as to become unrecognizable.

Articulating his view that India is no place for British niceties, Ronny Heaslop ironically reveals what happens to those—usually not England's best and brightest but those who for one reason or another are unlikely to excel in England—sent out to govern India or other colonies: "We're not out here for the purpose of behaving pleasantly!" (43). While Heaslop and his colleagues are referring to a country that they regard as chaotic and underdeveloped, Forster implies in his novel that the politics of imperialism and the concomitant imaginative failure of the English to understand India's people and culture are the source of much of the difficulty in India. But he does not minimize the cultural differences between Hindu and Muslim, or totally exculpate either of those cultures from responsibility.

Forster not only shows how the tradition of manners fails when it leaves the insularity of an English village, but hints at its obsolescence. We should recall that hierarchical relationships and a stifling class system have been a concern of Forster in his prior novels, *Where Angels Fear to Tread* (1905), *The Longest Journey* (1907), *A Room with a View* (1908), and *Howards End* (1910). Adela's poignant comment about a tradition of personal relationships may underline Forster's nostalgia for a time when personal relations flourished: "What is the use of personal relationships when everyone brings less and less to them?" (188). But her comment reminds us that Forster as homosexual outsider did not feel included in English personal relationships and felt the need to wear a social mask. It also reminds the resistant reader, aware of English class structure in the nineteenth and early twentieth century, that many others were also excluded.

While hardly rivaling Gandhi, Forster played an important role in raising British consciousness about the effects of colonialism and helped pave the way for British withdrawal. His writing—his novel-length passage of writing—provided eloquent testimony to how English ideals were corrupted by self-created imperialistic myths often based upon racist assumptions. The English and Indians are in an imperialistic relationship based on dominance and subservience. Members of both the conquering and conquered nation are corrupted and diminished when a relatively small number of representatives of the dominant nation willfully exercise power to keep the entire population of the subservient nation in humiliating circumstances.

For Forster, India is not only the setting for a novel, or even a metaphor for British imperialism, but an essential and troubling reality that he knows from personal experience.

The narrator tentatively adopts, seriatim, the perspectives of Fielding, Mrs. Moore, and Godbole as he is frustrated by searches not only for ways to alleviate the cultural and human gulf among Muslims, Hindus, and English, but also for a set of values to replace those that are dismayingly unsatisfactory in the face of what he is narrating. Thus we can say that whereas Austen's focus is on the moral development of her characters, Forster's is on making sense not only of the imagined world he has created but also of the real or anterior world that informs it.

Forster dramatizes the transformation of his surrogate, the narrator. As the narrator learns that evil is as much in the human psyche as in the Caves, he realizes the England of Austen's novels—the customs and manners she evokes—is irrelevant to India. The telling becomes a passage if not to enlightenment, at least to understanding. That Forster changes his values urges the narratee—the implied reader whom he addresses—to reconsider his own attitudes toward India; put another way, the narrator's transformation of values becomes part of the novel's rhetoric of persuasion.

Unlike Austen's Highbury in *Emma*, India is more than a background for events in an imagined world. For Forster, India represents passion, poetry, and sexuality, and thus offers the possibility of intimacy. India is often the novel's major character; as with Hardy's coming to terms with Sue or even Jude in *Jude the Obscure*, Forster's coming to terms with his character India is presented in a complicated and even contradictory way that reflects the author's ambivalence. One might say that the difference between Austen's Highbury and Forster's India is the difference between John Constable's eighteenth-century landscapes, depicting scenes such as Salisbury Cathedral as it might have looked at an ideal moment, and the landscapes of such post-Impressionists as Paul Cézanne and Vincent van Gogh, who express the emotions of the painter more than they depict the actual or even idealized physical scene.

When we open a novel we enter an imagined world with its own cosmology and grammar of motives. *A Passage to India* has one of the most wonderful openings in the English novel. Its first chapter dramatizes the grim schisms that divide India, separating it into different nations occupying the same space at the same time but divided along racial, ethnic, and religious grounds. Forster has invented the geography, for there is no Chandrapore along the Ganges; nor do the Caves he describes exist as the Marabar Caves.

In the first paragraph of Part One of the three-part novel, entitled "Mosque," Chandrapore is defined by the narrator—as if he were in the streets—in terms of what the city is *not*:

> Edged rather than washed by the river Ganges, it trails for a couple of miles along the bank, scarcely distinguishable from the rubbish it deposits so freely. There are no bathing-steps on the river front, as the Ganges happens not to be holy here; indeed there is no river front, and bazaars shut out the wide and shifting panorama of the stream. The streets are mean, the temples ineffective. […] The very wood seems made of mud, of mud moving. [… T]he general outline of the town persists, swelling here, shrinking there, like some low but indestructible form of life. (2)

Until the eighteenth century, Chandrapore had some stature but it seems to be in a long period of continuing decline. Those readers who know the awesome beauty of India's geography and historical sites will respond to the deliberate reductive bathos—what we might call the rhetoric of nullification dominated by words like "filth," "mud," and "low"—with which Forster describes this place. Within this India there seems to be no distinction between Muslim and Hindu.

But in the second paragraph the narrator, adopting a hawk's perspective and changing his optics to a view from above, introduces the reader to a different world; on the first rise are the houses of the Euro-Asians, and on the second the English rulers, and from their perspective Chandrapore looks entirely different: "It is a city of gardens. It is no city, but a forest sparsely scattered with huts. It is a tropical pleasance washed by a noble river" (3). Trees soar

> to build a city for birds. Especially after the rains do [the trees] screen what passes below, but at all times, even when scorched and leafless,

they glorify the city to the English people who inhabit the rise, so that
new-comers cannot believe it to be as meagre as it is described, and
have to be driven down to acquire disillusionment. (3)

But the civil station on the second rise is itself described by negatives
as if to emphasize its kinship with the land below and the people
which it suppresses—"It charms not"—and the best the narrator can
concede is that "It has nothing hideous in it" (3).

Within the first two paragraphs the narrator's perception of geography enacts the unbridgeable schism between the English and Indians,
imperialists and colonial subjects. The trialogue between the Ganges
River, vegetation, and sky—between the mud of Chandrapore, the
ordering gardens, and the indifferent cosmos—mirrors the trialogue
between three cultures that is the essence of the novel. Describing
the sky, the stars, and the sun, the last two paragraphs of the opening
chapter move to an even more distant perspective, one that anticipates
the narrator's cosmological perspective, which emphasizes the dimin-
utive nature of humans and their relatively short presence on earth
not merely as individuals but as a species.

The Caves become a metaphor for the timelessness of the geological cosmos and for the non-verbal world that preceded and will
outlast humankind. Like Hardy's Wessex geography, the Caves are
indifferent to human aspirations. His narrator's description reveals
Forster's imaginative effort and even personal agony. It is as if the
Caves resist human description even though we are told that they
are "readily described": "Nothing, nothing attaches to them and
their reputation—for they have one—does not depend upon human
speech" (117). On the one hand, the Caves depend upon oral and
written language for their reputation and their significance. On the
other hand, the very inadequacy of the language illustrates the mind's
limitations as it confronts the unknown.

By placing human events in a vast geological context, Forster reduces
their proportion.

Let us examine further the transformation of values within *A Passage
to India*. Initially Forster embraces the code of Fielding, the teacher
and liberal humanist who befriends Aziz. At first glance Fielding's

code would not be out of place in an Austen novel: "The world, he believed, is a globe of men who are trying to reach one another and can best do so by the help of goodwill plus culture and intelligence— a creed ill suited to Chandrapore, but he had come out too late to lose it" (56). Forster admires Fielding's self-control, decency, and fundamental courage (what he called "pluck" in the essay "What I Believe"). Fielding—the "holy man minus the holiness"—embodies the spirit of Bloomsbury's ideal of personal relationships. He is the epitome of liberal England, and the heir to the tradition of manners and morals: "I believe in teaching people to be individuals, and to understand other individuals. It's the only thing I do believe in" (132). But no sooner do we think that the narrator has adopted or even fully endorsed the values of Fielding than he steps back and re-examines them.

Although not recognizing the homosocial and latent homosexual feelings that draw him to Aziz, Fielding himself is at least dimly aware that he lacks Aziz's passionate intensity and intuitive generosity: "[Fielding] wished that he too could be carried away on waves of emotion" (109). Even though Forster later marries Fielding off, Fielding has no real interest in women and, indeed, "took no notice" of the wives of his colleagues (56). Nor does Forster acknowledge in his commentary that the attraction between Fielding and Aziz is mutual.

Even while *A Passage to India* provides a room with a view—to borrow from the title of Forster's 1908 novel set at first in Italy— Forster is redefining the equation of travel with learning and moral growth. That equation is an essential premise of much eighteenth- and nineteenth-century fiction and travel literature from *Moll Flanders* and *Tom Jones* to *Jane Eyre* and *Great Expectations*. The equation is a version of the Protestant myth of self-improvement through experience and hard work.

In *A Passage to India,* travel is equated for the English with education about the corrosive effects of imperialism. If we think of Fielding's self-image as a traveler, we realize the concept of traveling as an experience of learning but not necessarily growth or self-development is central to *A Passage to India*. Fielding's stature is reduced when he returns to England, marries, and becomes part of the hierarchy of English education in India, ironically proving his own contention that "Any man can travel light until he has a wife or children" (112).

Even before Aziz's trial, after Adela has wrongfully accused him of molesting her, Forster's narrator begins to separate himself from Fielding and to reveal that Fielding's values provide only a partial perspective on understanding India and that Fielding's truths are partial truths. For he shows us that Fielding lacks imagination, passion, and spiritual depth. We see this clearly when Fielding sees the Caves from a distance. Failing to apprehend the sublime if terrifying beauty of the Caves, he questions his life and values:

> After forty years' experience, he had learned to manage his life and make the best of it on advanced European lines, had developed his personality, explored its limitations, controlled his passions—and he had done it all without becoming either pedantic or worldly. A creditable achievement, but as the moment passed he felt he ought to have been working at something else the whole time—he didn't know at what, never would know, never could know, and that was why he felt sad. (181)

Forster's style parodies the self-control and balance of Fielding's mind. Words like "manage," "developed," "explored," and "controlled" capture the essence of the liberal humanist view that life can be understood and mastered as if it were a space—or colony—to be mapped, explored, and conquered. Fielding avoids the Scylla and Charybidis of worldliness and pedantry. Yet the last sentence of the aforementioned quotation opens to Fielding and the reader the possibility that something more exists; a series of inconclusive and imprecise clauses give way to recognition—indeed, a revelation—that his way is only one possible way and a limited one at that.

If I were to choose a paradigmatic vignette to show how Forster turns the novel of manners upside down, it would be this moment when he exposes the limitations of his erstwhile surrogate Fielding. Could we imagine Austen's Knightley in a moment of self-doubt, alone in a moral desert bereft of values? Finally, Fielding in India has no tradition of manners on which to rely; nor can he as an agnostic fall back on belief in a benevolent cosmos or the presence of God's Holy Plan. Fielding, we realize, is exposed and contained within a text in which, by tradition, he should be the hero. For has he not risked career and perhaps even his physical well-being in the interests of truth and fairness? Yet this apparently is not enough.

In his prior novels, Forster focused upon the plagues of moral relativism, materialism, and social snobbery, plagues which could be contained and perhaps partially controlled by the kind of values Fielding represents and articulates. But after the trial at which Aziz is exonerated, the narrator stresses that Fielding's liberal humanism is one of several possible sets of values. In the last part of "Caves" and in "Temple," Forster is not only questioning Fielding's values but the values to which he had dedicated his prior novels—the primacy of personal relationships and the necessity of understanding one another; these are the values epitomized by the famous epigraph to *Howards End*, "Only connect."

Yet finally in *A Passage to India* humanism triumphs, if in a reduced and more modest version. As Godbole and Mrs. Moore are tested and ultimately discarded as prophets, the narrative voice again becomes the spokesman for the values of humanism—moderation, tolerance, tact, integrity, and respect for others. The narrator's own language presents the unity and balance that life in India—perhaps life anywhere—lacks.

Despite Mrs. Moore's early empathy for Aziz, she ultimately deserts Aziz as she puts aside relations with people and withdraws into herself. After her experience in the Caves, she turns her back on human ties. While the narrator understands Mrs. Moore's impatience with life, he cannot endorse it because finally it involves selfish desertion of her friend Aziz. For Forster, spiritual self-realization cannot come at the expense of human relations. Indeed, he may be indicting the sanctimony of Christianity: "Her Christian tenderness had gone, or had developed into a hardness, a just irritation against the human race: she had taken no interest at the arrest, asked scarcely any questions" (190).

Her mythic identity as "Esmiss Esmoor" that she takes on for Indians—as if she were a kind of minor Hindu goddess—has nothing to do with her actual behavior. That her disdain for human relations

54

parallels Godbole's cosmic perspective is strongly ironic. Forster's characterization of Mrs. Moore is a wonderful and rare depiction of the process of the later stages of aging as subtraction from community and preparation for death. Her self-immersion represents a serious failure of the "connection"—to use Forster's term—that should bind one human to another. Whatever the excuse, does Mrs. Moore not commit what for Forster is the heresy of deserting her friend?

A fundamental paradox of the text is that Forster's own prose has difficulty aligning itself with unspoken mysteries and spiritual values. Yet the celebratory and performative religious ritual of "Temple" is an effort to move beyond the concatenation of events on which traditional western narrative is based. Within "Temple," we might (somewhat reductively) say that we can locate a double perspective: 1) the external perspective of a secular but open-minded skeptic, whose view, like Fielding's, is predicated on interest in other cultures and who earnestly desires to understand unfathomable mysteries of other cultures; 2) the inner vision of someone, who, like Godbole, is experiencing a revelation of the transcendent unity of the cosmos as he participates in the performance ritual of the birth of SHRI KRISHNA. (It is worth remembering that Krishna, the seventh incarnation of Vishnu, is with Rama one of the two Gods who embodies humanity and who, in the epic Mahabharata, is the god who intercedes on behalf of heroes.)

The dialectic between the echo in the cave—representing inexplicable evil and the absence of good—and the Hindu religion—representing a quest to transcend the individual by overcoming the limitations of space and time and unite with a universal soul—is central to Forster's effort to introduce what he calls "prophecy" in his *Aspects of the Novel*. In the ending to *A Passage to India*, Forster strives for "expansion" and "opening out" by which he means a movement that takes the reader beyond space and temporal limitations of narrative to a performative ecstasy: "Expansion. That is the idea that the novelist must cling to. Not completion. Not rounding off but opening out. When the symphony is over we feel that the notes and tunes composing it have been liberated, they have found in the rhythm of the whole their individual freedom" (Forster 1954, 116).

55

If Forster believes that works of art can reach for transcendence, he is much concerned when individuals wear the mantle of transcendence.

Godbole's stature as a prophetic figure is undermined by his human failures. As a Brahmin, he "had never been known to tell anyone anything" (295). He is no help to Aziz when he is falsely accused; later he allows Aziz to believe Fielding has married Adela when in fact Fielding has married Mrs. Moore's daughter. Aziz's misconception leads him into foolish and even humiliating behavior. Although Forster's narrator does at times take a geological and historical perspective that minimizes human presence as a small blip in time, the novel finally rejects Godbole's hawk's-eye view of human behavior or at the most sees it as one of discursive formation. According to Godbole: "Good and evil are different, as their names imply. But, in my humble opinion, they are both aspects of my Lord. He is present in the one, absent in the other" (169).

Just as Fielding's rationalism and control have their limits, so do Godbole's ascetic spirituality and his ability to thrust himself out of himself. With gentle irony, Forster examines the Hindu concept that supreme divinity can be found in any object by being worshipped at one moment by one particular person. For even Godbole cannot meditate upon the stone: "He loved the wasp equally, he impelled it likewise, he was imitating God. And the stone, where the wasp clung— could he [...] no, he could not, he had been wrong to attempt the stone, logic and conscious effort had seduced" (277).

Godbole's long view—his search for transcendence—seems to be patronizing if not dismissive of the manners and passions of individuals, and human life is what interests Forster. He views Godbole's spiritualism as another of humankind's working arrangements. The Hindu celebration is an outlet for very human and even animal passions and instincts. To perform the Rajah's holy journey after the Rajah dies, the Hindus simply—and to skeptical western eyes perhaps bathetically— make an effigy of the Rajah, but is that so different from the faith required to believe in the Eucharist? If at first the novel seems to reject Fielding's liberal humanism, it gradually shows that the alternatives are no better. That religion is not a living force binding humans to one another within a community is illustrated by Godbole's human failures. Like Mrs. Moore, he has subtracted himself from a human community in his search for something more. Thus Fielding's humanism may have a qualified triumph, after all, when we realize the effects of being "one with the universe" as exemplified by Mrs. Moore's and Godbole's indifference to other people (198).

Mrs. Moore's son Ralph is the western correlative to the "untouchable" Indian who turns the fan in the courtroom. Do not Ralph's simple vocabulary, depth of feeling, and intuitive understanding of Hindu rituals comment upon the verbosity of the Muslims and the complicated motives of the English? Although he "appeared almost an imbecile," Ralph instinctively understands Aziz's hostility; by telling Aziz that his mother loved him, he is the catalyst for Aziz's temporary, if tense, reconciliation with Fielding. And perhaps he anticipates Forster's final verdict—"not yet"—on the possibility of lasting reconciliation. That wisdom becomes the province of the unwitting in Ralph—and in several figures such as Emerson (*Room with a View*), Gino (*Where Angels Fear to Tread*), Stephen Wonham (*The Longest Journey*)—is an aspect of Forster's rebellion against utilitarianism, progress, and moral education.

Even if Forster's geography is an illuminating distortion, do we not from reading *Passage to India* anticipate much of what we will learn from visiting India and do we not better understand the divisions within India? But the reverse is also true; after visiting India we reread *Passage to India* with greater understanding. One reason for globalization of imagined literature stems from the accessibility of places earlier generations could never have dreamed of visiting. We want to read about exotic places, which we may visit or have visited.

After I visited India on a brief tour a few years ago, I began to understand the immensity and infinite variety and cultural complexity of India's history and people. While Hinduism is the dominant religion, the Muslim minority is the world's second-largest Muslim population. A few centuries before the English imposed their will upon India, the Muslims conquered India and established their own empire. Under the leadership of Mahatma Gandhi and

Jawaharlal Nehru, India freed itself from nearly two centuries of British domination after World War II and on January 26, 1950, became a fully independent country. India is now the world's largest democracy.

V. Reading Women: What We Learn about Women's (and Men's) Psyches from Reading Virginia Woolf

Virginia Woolf teaches us about being a woman in the early twentieth century, or more precisely, being a woman married to a man of some standing. In *Mrs. Dalloway*, Virginia Woolf has captured the agony of Clarissa's loneliness, the results of her sexual repression and frigidity, and her capitulation to social convention. Clarissa's life is a function of a few crucial decisions made years ago. In a sense, her life is over because she has missed her chance for love with both Peter and Sally and settled for something less. Clarissa feared intimacy with Peter because "everything had to be shared; everything gone into" (1925, 10); she chooses the separateness that culminates in the room in the attic to which she is consigned. Peter recalls that "there was always something cold in Clarissa" (73). Alternatively, had she responded to her impulse to love a woman, she might have been fulfilled that way. Repressed to the point of frigidity, she is both attracted to and frightened by the spontaneity of Peter and Sally. For her, giving parties provides the possibility of unity with others that her personal life lacks. She requires the admiration of others to complete her: "How much she wanted it—that people should look pleased as she came in" (13). The passivity of Clarissa, locked into her stereotypical social roles of aging hostess, supportive political wife, and household manager, contrasts with Peter, who remains alive and open to possibilities. Even as Peter confronts aging, disappointment, and loneliness, he lives and speaks according to his feelings.

The point of departure for Woolf is Jane Austen's world of English country houses, rigid social customs, and understated feelings and attitudes. In *A Room of One's Own* (1920) Woolf contends that prior to nineteenth-century fiction written by women, men always show women in their relation to men [...] and how small a part of woman's life is that; and how little can a man know even of that when he observes it through the black or rosy spectacles which sex puts upon his nose. Hence, perhaps, the peculiar nature of woman in fiction; the astonishing extremes of her beauty and horror, her alternations between heavenly goodness and hellish depravity. (*Room*, 86)

By contrast, when a middle-class woman such as Austen, Emily Brontë, or George Eliot wrote, she wrote novels because she was trained "in the observation of character, in the analysis of emotion. Her sensibility had been educated for centuries by the influences of the common sitting-room. People's feelings were impressed on her; personal relations were always before her eyes" (*Room*, 70).

Woolf focuses on the individual moments of heightened perceptions, although she does not neglect the physical details of daily life or the historical or economic contexts. For her, "reality" does include a keen awareness of World War I, and the permanent change it wrought in England's social fabric.

To the Lighthouse enables Woolf to come to terms with the burden of her past, particularly her dominant father and her elusive but sensitive mother. In probing the needs and desires of the Ramsays and their guests, Woolf reminds us how the quirks and idiosyncrasies of those who can channel their energies into socially acceptable directions (the masterful but insensitive Mr. Ramsay, in particular) are not so different from the fantasies and delusions of those whom society chooses to regard as mad pariahs, such as Septimus Smith. But most of all, *To the Lighthouse* enabled Woolf to inquire into the relationship between art and life as well as between memory and experience, and to show how artistic creation is related to the ordering and distorting qualities of memory. Do not memory and artistic creativity both depend upon the mind's ability to create meaning from the past and to inform the present with insights that such meaning can provide?

Woolf teaches us about striking dichotomies in the world in which she was raised, although she transfers them to her imagined ontology. In Woolf's memory, it is her mother who provided fecundity and energy, who attended to the children's needs, who made life bearable in a house in which an oppressive, larger-than-life, famous father dominated. In a dualism that recalls the dichotomy D.H. Lawrence draws between male and female qualities, Mrs. Ramsay represents the subjective—feelings, personal relationships, the possibility of discovering meaning and even unity, if only temporarily. For the children, her husband, the young couple, Charles Tinsley, William Bankes, and Lily, Mrs. Ramsay is a kind of minor deity. Thus she has the capacity to create rapture in Mr. Bankes: "[T]he sight of her reading a fairy tale to her boy had upon him precisely the same effect as the solution of a scientific problem so that he rested in contemplation of it, and felt [...] that barbarity was tamed, the reign of chaos subdued" (74). By contrast, Mr. Ramsay represents objective facts, recognition of life's difficulties, achievements, ambition, and enterprise.

That Mrs. Ramsay remembers a day twenty years ago as if it were yesterday stresses the importance of memory in giving shape to the very day that the characters are living (and the importance to the rereader of his memory of his first reading of *To the Lighthouse*). Mrs. Ramsay regrets that James "will remember all his life" his father's prophesy about the weather on the day at age six when he planned to go to the lighthouse (132). In Part III, Lily, by making sense of her past experience at the Ramsay house, is trying to discover significance in her present life and art. As in Proust, memory triggers complex emotions about people. For William Bankes the dunes become an elegiac moment for the friendship he once had with Ramsay: "[T]here, like the body of a young man laid in peat for a century, with the red fresh on his lips, was his friendship, in its acuteness and reality, laid up across the bay among the sandhills" (35); the trace of mortality is always present in memory and in art. *To the Lighthouse* is an attempt to immortalize such moments and to unify them into one grand experience. That is why the book stresses memories of experience frozen in time by the mind and why the act of perception is the object of memories and the narrative.

The entire novel revolves around a contest between death and life, order and flux, creative imagination and the "scraps and fragments" of ordinary experience (136). No sooner does Mrs. Ramsay or Lily experience unity than "there was a sense of things having been blown apart, of space, of irresponsibility" (111). *To the Lighthouse* is a novel which is about the very processes of creating meaning from inchoate personal experience. The struggle for order and meaning within each of the characters' lives is not only the central action of the novel, but the activity that engaged Woolf herself. Doesn't Woolf's own art mime Lily's struggles to render what she sees rather than merely what convention dictates? Woolf's narrator comments: "It was in that moment's flight between the picture and [Lily's] canvas that the demons set on her who often brought her to the verge of tears and made this passage from conception to work as dreadful as any down a dark passage for a child" (32).

Style and form teach us; in *To the Lighthouse* they enact and affirm the principles of order, sensibility, and discrimination that Mrs. Ramsay lives by. But the possibility of disorder, insensitivity, and personal failure are always threatening to intrude into the novel's imagined world. In "her strange severity, her extreme courtesy," her refusal to "regret her decision, evade difficulties, or slur over duties," Mrs. Ramsay not only represents a queenly presence in the social world, a presence that provides standards for others, but also a concept of order which has its correlative in the tight design of the book's structure and texture (14). Yet the process by which the consciousness of characters even within a day, even an hour, oscillates between feelings of unity and disunity creates a tension between formal coherence and the possibility that life lacks meaning. Lily's or Mrs. Ramsay's despair at one moment is given meaning by the ecstasy of a subsequent one, and vice versa. Like Woolf herself, the characters often live at the edge of desperation, even madness.

VI. Learning from Nadine Gordimer's *The Pickup*

Let us take as our example of how more recent books with a political focus teach us Nadine Gordimer's *The Pickup* (2001), Cornell's 2007 freshmen reading project text. At the most obvious level, the title takes its name from what happens when a dark-skinned auto mechanic Abdu (later Ibrahim)—an illegal alien from an unnamed Third World country who has found work because he is cheaper labor than the residents—is picked up casually in Johannesburg by a wealthy young white South African woman named Julie; she is rebelling against her family's materialism. She is attracted to the exoticism of Abdu and he to the possibility that she can be a bridge to remaining in the country. The narrator makes clear that Abdu is not an innocent and that he is aware of the possibility that Julie could help him stay in South Africa because of her ties to the rich and powerful.

Gordimer also takes us to an unnamed Middle Eastern country where feudal customs and modern life clash, but where Julie— by choosing to accompany Abdu after he is deported from South Africa—becomes an immigrant in a town surrounded by desert. Thus we see both Abdu and Julie in alien cultures. Gordimer's novel depends upon rendering the very different perspectives of Julie and Abdu as each responds to their own culture as well as to the culture they have picked up by involving themselves in the world of the other.

The Pickup shows us the warp and woof of two cultures quite different from America in 2007. It examines what it is like to be a stranger in a land where one is not recognized for whom he is, and it shows us how a person sees himself in part as a function of how others see him.

Meaning, as we shall see, revolves around a number of key words and phrases. While Abdu is extraordinarily determined and finally arranges to go legally to the United States, he never casts off his self-image as a "penniless illegal"—even though he has a university degree—after he returns to his own country (*The Pickup*, 173). He thinks of the period of living in his own country, as "In the meantime they happened to be living through." In his own country, he "set[s] himself passionately adrift" against "the bonds of life." By contrast, Julie takes great pains to reinvent herself as something other than the spoiled daughter of wealthy entrepreneur Nigel Summers and tries to become a woman in a culture where women are defined by their domestic tasks and their functionality. For Julie, the desert is epitomized by the word "always" and comes to stand for a longer if not eternal view of time that is indifferent to human life.

Abdu (known as Ibrahim in his native land) detests his country; carved out by western cartographers, it is poor, corrupt, backward, and without oil. He is disappointed that he has been rejected by the west and that he has not fulfilled his dream of providing economic support to his mother, father, and siblings. When he returns to his native country, his every effort is focused on emigrating. He has little interest in using his degree from an Arab university to engage in national politics and to try to change his own country. His alienation from his own world and his envy of western life gives us a clue into radical Islamic politics, although his determination and individualism take him on another path. He thinks his proudest moment is rejecting his uncle's offer to take charge of the latter's automobile repair shop; Abdu believes, were he to do so, he would be accepting living his life in his home country.

Gordimer's text is built on contrasts. In Gordimer's presentation of South Africa, a crucial contrast is the vast schism between the wealthy and the poor, and we see that with a few notable exceptions such as Mr. Hamilton Motsami—who formerly was involved in defending blacks but whose behavior now mimics the white oligarchs— blacks have not established a place at the high table of capitalism. Most still do the menial work for the whites; even though Julie lives in a modest under-furnished cottage rather than in the suburbs she detests, a black woman does her laundry.

Like Julie, many of the younger people in Johannesburg are alien- ated and straddle a position between the capitalist culture and bohe- mian culture—epitomized by the racial mixed group who sit at the Table at the El-Ay café—which seems more hedonistic (and work-averse) than idealistic. The Table's deracinated inhabitants seem only to belong to their cynical alternative culture and to be paralyzed by talk and sloth as well as a mixture of drugs and alcohol. Interestingly, many of the bohemians at the Table think Abdu is Indian because that would make him fit into one—Indian—of the vestigial categories of Apartheid, which ended in 1990.

In an October 23, 2003, *New York Review* piece, J.M. Coetzee remarks:

With an expensive education and some business experience behind her, a trust fund in her name, and a mother married to a wealthy

American, Julie could easily acquire residence in the United States; Ibrahim could then—in the world of *The Pickup,* the world as it was before September 11, 2001—come as her spouse.

But Julie won't give Abdu this bridge, either from misplaced fear that he will fail in the United States about which she has a myopic view or from her naive view of the desert world.

Julie turns her back not only on western acquisitiveness, which still supports her, but also on the post-Apartheid bohemian life that she has adopted. At least as much as Abdu has been able to adapt to western life, she adapts to a far more primitive culture in a small village living according to customs established generations ago. Julie's identity in the desert is "Ibrahim's wife" or "a woman" or "this girl," but she comes to enjoy the simple routines of life in the house of his family. She feels a tie to Abdu's mother—whom he respects, unlike Julie who oscillates between coolness and disdain for her parents. Indeed, she is Julie's ally for her own purposes, thinking that if her son stays in her house to be with his wife, she will fully regain her son.

Who is, finally, "The Pickup"? Is it Julie who was has been picked up by an alien desert culture with which she now feels comfortable? For "the meantime" has turned into her life, and she has no intention of leaving with Abdu and watching him build a life based on menial jobs in what she thinks of as "the harshest country in the world" and of taking part in the tradition embedded in both western and this desert culture of following her man. He wants her to go live with her well-to-do mother because at first as an immigrant doing basic workman jobs at the bottom of the economic ladder, "You are a stray dog, a rat finding its hole as the way to get in" (226). She refuses, but she will presumably be in his home village for him if he chooses or needs to return: "I am not going anywhere. […] I am in your home" (261). She has found purpose in teaching English and a place among his family.

To be picked up implies having fallen down, and we learn in different ways that both Julie and Abdu believe they have fallen down. She is an insider in a culture she regards as bankrupt or fallen down, and she wants to emigrate to a different set of values represented by the desert and the matriarchal culture of Abdu's household; he is an illegal who wants to leave the values of his country and find another life. He has been picked up not only by Julie, but also by western values; in fact, he admires her father's acquisitive values, which she detests. He detests being picked up by the ancient values of his impoverished Arab homeland. We wonder if she will find the oasis she seeks without the eroticism and romance she had when Abdu is with her there—and which are extremely important to her. And does he have the technical and personal skills to survive in America?

Finally Gordimer's narrative seems to affirm an idea of female independence at odds with its own ethos of romantic and erotic love as the inspiration for behavior on both their parts. For Abdu and Julie, "another country"—which they inhabit together—is that of sexual and romantic love. That country of sexual compatibility is a Brigadoon away from both the trials of South Africa and the unnamed Middle Eastern country.

What else does the novel teach us? For one thing, the novel shows us the political tensions within post-Apartheid South Africa, a nation full of promise and beset by difficulties as it tries to chart an interracial future. For another, it dramatizes the inequality and arbitrariness of immigration procedures. Finally, it gives us a window into how life is lived in remote byways of the Third World. But it also teaches us about the thin line that divides self-delusion from self-awareness, sentiment from passion, and community from inverted narcissism.

Gordimer ask her readers to join Julie in a visit backwards in time, but we somewhat resist her invitation because Gordimer seems to have a romanticized view of what Julie's life in the desert will be. To be sure, Julie does seem to feel some commonality with the Arab women and enjoys the simplicity of their life, fetching water, cooking food, taking part in hospitality rituals, and following simple routines awaiting the return of the males from their workdays. Will she take her place with other women in a world where women seem subservient in tasks but perhaps not influence? What kind of life is she buying into fetching water, cooking for the men, living without the man she had chosen, and without sex which has been so important to her? Without husband and children, will she be a supernumerary?

And where is the narrator in all this? At first we see things through Julie's eyes but gradually we also see from Abdu's perspective. With Abdu, we wonder whether Julie is simply a rolling stone on another adventure. Abdu lives in his own country with his "never completely unpacked" "canvas bag standing ready that carried his life from country to country" (148, 151). He believes "that privilege can never be brought to understanding of reality, of what matters, the dignity of survival against principles" (223).

Yet do we ever have an independent narrative view except in the careful selection and arrangement of incident, dialogue, characterization, setting, and plot? In a nineteenth-century novel we would have more narrative commentary and direction and we would understand the ironic distinctions between the characters' views and the narrator's. By contrast, in modernist and postmodernist texts, we need to rely on our sense-making to interpret the author's presentation of character. Our learning is dependent on the interaction between what the narrator shows us and our own perspective, but we should not minimize how much control skillful authors have over what we learn.

Does it not seem that Gordimer's narrator is being ironic and expects us to see that Julie lacks self-awareness? But sometimes the irony wobbles and we are not sure where the voice stands, and this inability to present a completely clear view of a complex situation is part of the aporia of postmodernism and an inadvertent part of our learning experience. We realize Julie partakes of a romantic western dream about the purity of the desert that goes back through T.E. Lawrence— for whom she has contempt even while romanticizing it very much as Lawrence had—to Disraeli's *Tancred*. Isn't Julie's daily walk to the desert part of a western tendency to romanticize the desert as eternal—that is, as something that precedes and perhaps succeeds human life—while forgetting that sand without water is in fact resistant to most life? We realize that Julie is always an outsider to the mother's Muslim faith as well as the faith of the other believers. As we come to understand what Julie's naive exoticism—she embraces the desert, while Abdu "shuns" the desert as "the denial of everything he yearns for"—we also begin to question Julie's decision to remain behind.

I want to close my discussion of *The Pickup* with a brief comment on how our own personal experience informs our reading and vice versa. We all come to books with different experiences and prior reading. None us is a blank slate. In 2005 I visited South Africa and have done some reading in its history and imaginative literature—and had a fair number of émigré friends—and this background increases my awareness of the novel's political implications.

Although the South African capitalist culture has much in common with other corporate cultures, the racial history of that country hovers over every moment just as it never leaves Gordimer's text. To understand South Africa one needs to understand Apartheid, a political system by which the ruling white minority in 1948 divided people into four racial groups: white, black (the vast majority), colored or mixed race, and Indian. The word *Apartheid* is the Afrikaans word for segregation and it describes a policy in which racial classification determined where one could live and work and with whom one could have intimate relations. Blacks who actively opposed the system—many of whom belonged to Nelson Mandela's group, the African National Congress—were imprisoned and whites who opposed it with some exceptions were marginalized. The Sharpeville massacres took place in 1960, and a major revolt in the form of the Soweto Uprising took place in 1976. While the latter was an important catalyst in Apartheid's demise, the system really began to crumble in the 1980s but didn't end until Mandela's release from prison in 1990.

When I visited Johannesburg in summer 2005, that city was beset by enormous difficulties, and I have no reason to believe it has changed. Johannesburg had collapsed as a functioning city and its white population had fled to the suburbs. Ugly mountains of mine tailings (waste) surrounded the city. And the city itself was not safe. With its boarded-up hotels and shops, its hoards of unemployed men mingling aimlessly and its street debris, most of the areas in downtown Johannesburg, looked like the worst American city streets in the late 1960s. I kept thinking of a line in Alan Paton's *Cry, the Beloved Country* (1948); when a character, looking to the future, says something about South Africa building more cities like Johannesburg, the narrator comments that one is enough.

Notwithstanding its disgraceful past and current difficulties, the Republic of South Africa shows the promise of being an economically viable multiracial society and the hope of the continent. But there are major problems. South Africa has experienced a brain- and wealth-drain by whites who fear the majority black government won't have a place for them. We see this in the wealthy émigré to Australia, and in Julie's mother's settling with her American husband in the United States.

VII. How We Learn from Holocaust Literature

Let us turn to literature about the Holocaust, a literature that has been often written with a strong pedagogical function. Many readers know the basic facts, but the biographies, diaries, and imaginative literature open doors and windows into our understanding.

Holocaust literature depends on the power of content and many of its notable texts depend on aesthetic minimalism. Many Holocaust writers adhere to a kind of minimalism—to, as Raul Hilberg puts it, "the art of using the minimum of words to say the maximum" ("I Was Not There," Lang 1988, 23); they avoid trivialization and respect the need for silence. As I have argued, the tension between speaking and silence, between reclaiming life by means of language and images in the face of stories of extermination and torture, is a recurring theme of Holocaust narratives and a crucial component of their forms. In his essay "After the Holocaust," Aharon Appelfeld has written that "the problem, and not only the artistic problem, has been to remove the Holocaust from its enormous, inhuman dimensions and bring it close to human beings" (92). Unlike other art, which requires intensification, he argues that the Holocaust "seems so thoroughly unreal" that we "need to bring it down to the human realm" (92). In a version of the suffering, lamentation, and redemption in Jewish biblical and actual history, shtetl Jews learned that falling down and getting up needed to be one motion if they were to survive. Thus it is not surprising that Holocaust texts tell of individuals reclaiming their private identity and imagination, and that reclamation is a secularization of the traditional redemption topoi.

The intelligibility of history, even the place of evil in history, depends on reconfiguring it in imaginative and aesthetic terms. Many Holocaust texts encode catastrophe without resort to apocalyptic visions. Writers as diverse as Primo Levi, Elie Wiesel, Aharon Appelfeld, Tadeusz Borowski, John Hersey, and, yes, Anne Frank and Jerzy Kosinski all understand that, as Lawrence Langer puts it, "the Holocaust does little to confirm theories of moral reality but much to question the reality of moral theories" (1975, 198). They understand with Langer, "Auschwitz permanently destroyed the potency of the sedative we call illusion" (Langer 1991, 4). All of these writers understand how we domesticate the implausible and unthinkable into experiences within our ken. What these works have in common is brevity, a spare style, and a childlike vision of the adult world, an ingenuousness through which horrors are realized, the desire to humanize an experience without losing its mythic quality, and a structural principle that ostentatiously highlights and foregrounds some episodes at the expense of others. Each traces the gradual devolution of an organic community in the face of the Nazi parasite.

Most of the Holocaust texts—whether biographical or imaginative—begin in a pedestrian world of apparent normalcy, within a seemingly stable culture. What follows is usually a progressive narrative of disruption and deterioration, an unweaving of the strands of the individual and cultural constructions that make ordinary life what it is, until Jews are faced with unspeakable horrors of hunger, starvation, deportation, disease, crematoriums, and death marches. In Wiesel's case the very emphasis on graphic details paradoxically creates the fabric of a dreamscape. It is as if imagining the Holocaust requires metaphors and parables. Of course, different writers choose different approaches. Wiesel's *Night* and Primo Levi's *Survival at Auschwitz* are memoirs, but they exist on the borderland between fact and fiction. In each, the artist shapes his vision into a coherent form, highlighting some episodes that have value in terms of his structure, while discarding or giving minimal attention to others.

The imaginative energy of Holocaust fictional narratives—texts that transmute facts within the crucible of art into compelling forms—has become more and more a prominent part of how the collective memory of the Holocaust is shaped and survives. As the Holocaust Museum in Washington, DC, shows us, it is when Holocaust history is personalized and dramatized, when abstractions and numbers give way to human drama, that the distance between us and the victims closes. In a sense Holocaust narratives rescue language from its perversion in such terms as "final solution" or the sign over the inside of the Auschwitz gates "Arbeit Macht Frei" ("Work will make you free")—an obscene falsehood suggesting that the purpose of the concentration camp was to reform inmates who would then earn their freedom. As Langer observes, "the habit of verbal reassurance, through a kind of internal balancing act, tries to make more manageable for an uninitiated audience (and the equally uninitiated author?) impossible circumstances" (1991, 2).

While *The Diary of Anne Frank*, *Night*, and *Survival at Auschwitz* established the high seriousness and intense attention to the actual facts that we expect if not require of Holocaust narratives, Appelfeld's mocking fables, Art Spiegelman's comics, Leslie Epstein's caricatures and dreamscapes, and Andre Schwarz-Bart's use of myth and legend to structure his narrative are all departures from traditional naturalism and realism. Paradoxically their very efforts to depart from mimesis break down and show how the searing reality of the Holocaust resists these innovative forms. And it is this tension between putative formal solutions and inchoate resistance that is at the very center of these authors' artistic accomplishment. These more experimental authors acknowledge that representing the Holocaust—like all narrative representations—is a fiction, an illuminating distortion. But paradoxically, their reversion to documentary techniques—for example, the unexpected photographs in Spiegelman's graphic novel, *Maus*—and specific detailed testimony of the death camps demonstrate an inner resistance to aesthetic decisions that undermine realism or solemnity; they may fear—perhaps unconsciously—that such aesthetic decisions risk dishonoring the dead and trivializing the Holocaust.

It may be that Holocaust narratives enable us to enter into the subjective world of participants and to respond to historical events from their perspective. By walking in their shoes, sharing their pain and fear within the hypothesis "as if," the reader of Holocaust texts lives uniquely in fictive universes. The limits of our language, Wittgenstein taught us, are the limits of the world; the search for fictions to render the Holocaust, the quest for form and meaning, is different in degree but not kind from other artistic quests, and it does no dishonor to memory to say so. If the Nazis succeeded in turning words either into charred bone and flesh or skeletons that survived in terror— bodies almost completely deprived of their materiality—then writing about the Holocaust paradoxically restores the uniqueness of the human spirit by restoring the imaginative to its proper place and breathes new life into the materiality of victims and survivors. Were the victims to remain numb and mute, they would remain material without soul as well as participate in an amnesia that protected the culprits.

Before concluding this section, let us turn to Spiegelman's *Maus*. By using cartoon figures to present the Holocaust, Spiegelman creates in his *Maus* books a wildly inventive bibliocosm that invites us to look on the major topoi of the Holocaust from a radically different formal perspective. Mice are Spiegelman's vehicles for exploring the twentieth-century history of Europe from 1935 to 1945 and his own history as a survivor's son from 1948, his birth year. Art the narrator is not only Spiegelman's surrogate but a reminder of the role of art in making sense of the Holocaust as well as his father's life and his own.

As we read volume one we become accustomed to a world in which the Jews as mice live among Poles—who are depicted as pigs but are seldom seen except in a barely sketched background in one frame of the first chapter of volume one, a chapter which concerns private life leading up to his father's marriage, February 14, 1937.

Does not depicting the Jews as mice emphasize their position as Others, as those consigned to live apart in their mouse holes? As Spiegelman depicts the mice in bed or at dinner, we become accus-tomed to them as illuminating distortions that speak as humans. Gradually we accept that these mice with human features beneath their heads—except for tails, usually hidden by clothes—think, feel, love, as if they were humans. For they are! They retain the humanity that the Germans—who labeled them "vermin" and sought to "exter-minate" them—wished to deprive them of. Perhaps the absence of tails at first tellingly indicates that the metamorphosis is progressive; until we see swastikas on cats, there are no mice tails. The pictures and words combine to create a subtle psychology of character worthy of a modern novel. Unlike the mice in Disney cartoons that are buffeted by disaster and come back to life again and again, we soon realize that these mice stay dead.

Even as Spiegelman's characters see themselves as human, we see them as mice and cats within an imagined world where different nationalities are presented as different animals. Spiegelman's black-and-white frames, his lack of nominalistic detail in facial expressions and shapes, and the sparseness of dialogue paradoxically invites the experienced reader to fill in details by drawing upon his or her own experience of the Holocaust, while presenting the crystallizing themes in lucid and graphic form to those who are less knowledgeable. Spiegelman varies his style from the understated style that matches his father's rather understated anesthetized tone to the expressionist hyperbole and manic energy of the insert entitled "Prisoner on the Hell Planet" (1986a, 100–3) which depicts Spiegelman himself in a mental hospital after his mother dies and shows him wearing the pajama outfit of concentration camp inmates.

Not only are the characters in the insert humans but the insert also includes a photograph of Art and his mother on vacation in 1958. The occasional photographs not only reconnect the figures to our human world, but also deliberately call attention to the creative intelligence behind the metaphoricity of the mouse trope. In volume two Spiegelman includes photographic inserts of his brother Richieu (in the dedication) and, at the end, of his father in the pajama camp uniform. Spiegelman stresses that the picture of Vladek—taken after his release when he had returned to physical health—is staged in a souvenir shop in front of a curtain, and is, like his own cartoons, an illuminating distortion, a performance.

In its use of comic book forms, *Maus* is experimental, postmodern, and radical. Why do the characters wearing animal masks move us? Why does the carnivalesque nature of cartoon reality and the implied mockery of the hegemonic pretensions of human superiority successfully realize the Holocaust in such diverse works as Appelfeld's *Badenheim*

1939 and Epstein's *King of the Jews* as well as *Maus*? Yet, when laughing, do we not feel complicit with the perpetrators? Do we not as readers—and especially those of us who are Jewish readers—occupy a moral borderland in which we are the crossing guards, the *Judenrat*? Finally, are not the *Maus* books effective in part because they upset us in their form as well as content?

That Art captures his father's spoken testimony on a tape recorder is, like the photographs, part of the documentary nature of *Maus*; we realize that the cartoons, along with the photographs, and his father's oral testimony (and his own to the psychiatrist) are Spiegelman's way of presenting a complicated, multi-faceted view of his father's and his own life. Except for the striking title, the cover pages, and the introductory material, for much of the time it may seem as if words take precedence over images as we become accustomed to Spiegelman's basic trope of the Jews as mice. Yet, as we read, we never forget the images.

Indeed, often it is the drawings that teach us more than the written text. An example is the overpowering visual images in the segment in *Maus* where the cartoonist-narrator, obviously a surrogate for Spiegelman, depicts himself in clothing that suggests his father's concentration-camp clothing. By dressing Art in concentration-camp garb, Spiegelman shows that Art has transformed his psyche into an imprisoning camp and emphasizes how the son has transferred the position of victim to himself. Clearly he conflates his terrifying memory of the state mental hospital—he, like his mother, has been institutionalized at one point—with his father's memory of concentration camps. This is a visual example of how Art's trauma finds external confirmation for his own inner chaos. The last word of volume one is Art's muttering "Murderer" to himself as an accusation to his father for destroying his mother's diaries which he takes as metonymy for the father's not taking care of his fragile mother and driving her to suicide by his unreasonable demands (1986a, 159).

Another example of the preeminence of the visual is when Art presents himself in 1987, after the success of *Maus I* and five years after the 1982 death of his father. The cartoonist-narrator feels very small and depicts himself as metamorphosing in stages into a tiny infantile child mouse ("I want—I want—my Mommy!" [1986b, 42]); he retains that size when he visits his psychiatrist. In his insecurity after the publishing triumph of volume one, Art doubts himself and feels not like a Jew but like a person posing as a Jew. In the scene where he is a dwarf mouse in the psychiatrist's office, both he and the psychiatrist wear masks. We might recall the visual rendering of the Beckett-like dialogue between the psychiatrist—himself a Czech Jew and survivor of Terezin and Auschwitz—when he depicts himself as little mouse boy of about 3 in a big chair. His miniature version of his mouse self exclaims: "Samuel Beckett once said: 'Every word is like an unnecessary stain on silence and nothingness'" (1986b, 45). Following a frame in which the two smoke in hilarious self-absorbed silence, in the next frame Art looks up and says: "On the other hand, he SAID it" (1986b, 45). Doesn't this dialogue remind us of the power of words to invade silence and nothingness and give them meaning? Like other Holocaust literature, isn't Spiegelman responding to Adorno's famous dictum, "After Auschwitz to write a poem is barbaric" (Howe 1986, 28)?

VIII. Conclusion

We are what we read and we learn from art. From each reading experience—whether it be *Hamlet*, Stevens' "The Idea of Order at Key West," or Eliot's "The Love Song of J. Alfred Prufrock"—we learn something about how humans live and how artists make sense of their own world. And this is no less true for me when I visit museums or go to operas. When art raises questions about our core assumptions, it makes us rethink who we are.

Finally, as I have been implying, our reading odysseys are enriched when we learn how people behave in different times and circumstances. We understand the effects of Catholicism on a young Irish boy by reading "Araby" and how a middle-class Jew manages to preserve his humanity in *Ulysses* by his subscribing to ancient virtues of generosity, courage, and love. Forster's *A Passage to India* helps us understand the different value-systems that shape India; rigidity and nostalgia for the past anticipate the underlying issues in Deepa Mehta's contemporary film trilogy about India entitled *Air*, *Earth*, and *Water*. We shall understand from the spare eloquence of Wiesel's *Night*, as well as from the wonderful connection between words and images in Spiegelman's graphic novel *Maus*, the horrors that the Nazis inflicted on Jews in the Holocaust. We shall have insight about the history of women in England by reading Austen's *Pride and Prejudice*, Brontë's *Jane Eyre*, and Woolf's *Mrs. Dalloway*.

While what texts we value is a matter of personal choice, is it possible to claim one artistic work is more important than another because it gives more people greater pleasure even as it opens up the world to us in more complex ways? I am arguing in the affirmative. The value of a work of art is far more than as a cultural product, dependent on race, class, gender, ethnicity, and geography. Thus syllabi—and our own private reading lists—are not simply maps of a teacher's taste but can be astute selections of texts as windows into cultural traditions and values that are not only worth preserving but essential to living in our world.

By awakening our imagination, art intensifies and complements our own experience. Art represents people, cultures, values, and perspectives on living, but it does much more. It teaches us while bringing us pleasure because while reading or contemplating a painting our minds go elsewhere, take a journey into a world where form and meaning are intertwined. And that journey is what I call the odyssey of reading.

3

Towards a Community of Inquiry: Is There a Teacher in the Class?

I. Prologue

Let me begin with a codicil. Any proposal about what makes effective teaching should certainly be met with great skepticism. Whether one can make suggestions that cut across disciplines is ever more problematic. In this brief essay, I shall focus on one aspect of my teaching—the freshman writing seminar—since that is a widely shared experience. Nevertheless, much of what I have to say underlies my teaching philosophy at every level, including my undergraduate lecture course on modernism, my honors seminars, my senior seminars on Joyce's *Ulysses* and Holocaust literature, and even my graduate seminars.

Often when students say they don't like a book, they mean they don't understand it and/or they haven't finished it or they have read it quickly, skimming parts. It is our job as teachers to open up the book so they do understand it and to give it the reading it deserves.

A background note: I have been teaching a course entitled English 270, *The Reading of Fiction* for many of my forty years at Cornell. It is one of three 200-level courses offered by the English department; the others are English 271, *The Reading of Poetry*, and English 272, *The Reading of Drama*. Currently the 270 classes are reserved in the first term for those entering freshmen who have had a "4" or "5" on the Education Testing Service AP test in English Language or English Literature, or those entering freshmen who have scored "700" or better on the English Composition or English Achievement SAT tests. In the second term, the 270 classes are open to those who have taken a freshman seminar program, but the students understand from fellow students and advisors that these 270-level classes are more demanding and in the second term the principle of self-selectivity works well. Often the second term 270 classes have included a few students who begin their freshman year in January.

The students in the 270 classes rarely need remedial writing help. Most come from the College of Arts and Sciences and many are thinking about majoring in literature or related fields. Even in the second term most have had AP English in high school, and while a few in the second term have received a "3" or did not take either of the relevant AP tests, most have received at least a "4."

Under the current ethos, each 270 section has different reading materials. Originally the course had a common reading list, and that common list encouraged colleagues to discuss pedagogical issues including how to integrate the teaching of reading and writing. I would prefer to return to this, or at least have half of the reading in common. Not only do the teaching staff learn from one another when they teach a common syllabus, but, according to recent data, so do students taking common courses learn from discussing the material. The balkanization of the 270 syllabi—and indeed in the syllabi of the various sections of other courses in the Cornell writing program—is a development that I believe should be arrested.

When I was part of the original group developing English 270 in 1968 with much of a common syllabi, we used earlier editions of Robert Gorham Davis's *Ten Modern Masters* and Irving Howe's *Classics of Modern Fiction*, and while I have tried other collections, I prefer these—both of which have changed a great deal as they went from edition to edition. My section of English 270 reads sophisticated modern fiction: Joseph Conrad, D.H. Lawrence, James Joyce, Virginia Woolf, William Faulkner, Anton Chekhov, Fyodor Dostoevsky, Franz Kafka, and Thomas Mann. I characteristically begin with short stories by such figures as Ernest Hemingway, Joyce and Chekhov, but begin to integrate short novels such as Conrad's *The Secret Sharer,* Joyce's *The Dead*, Dostoevsky's *Notes from Underground*, and Kafka's *Metamorphosis,* and towards the end of the semester read one full-length novel, recently Conrad's *The Secret Agent* or Woolf's *To the Lighthouse*; over the years I have used as the full-length novel Dostoevsky's *Crime and Punishment,* Lawrence's *Sons and Lovers*, or Conrad's *Lord Jim*. I include some more relatively recent stories by writers such as Eudora Welty and Bernard Malamud.

I also have the students buy M.H. Abrams's *Glossary of Literary Terms,* William Strunk Jr. and E.B. White's *The Elements of Style*, and the *Harbrace College Handbook*. The students enjoy the Cornell flavor that the first two of the aforementioned books by Cornell authors bring to the course. In the first two-thirds of the course I assign from Abrams about five crucial terms per week.

II. Teaching Goals

Let us take as our point of departure George Orwell's remarks in his deservedly famous essay "Politics and the English Language":

> Most people who bother with the matter at all would admit that the English language is in a bad way, but it is generally assumed that we cannot by conscious action do anything about it. Our civilization is decadent and our language—so the argument runs—must inevitably share in the general collapse. It follows that any struggle against the abuse of language is a sentimental archaism, like preferring candles to electric light or hansom cabs to aeroplanes. Underneath this lies the half-conscious belief that language is a natural growth and not an instrument which we shape for our own purposes. (Orwell 1954, 162)

How many times have we heard versions of Orwell's comment by those who despair of the current condition, while lamenting that they once lived in the land of giants of language where they and their students wrote wonderfully sculpted prose? Yet my teaching experience does not validate that gloomy conclusion. What I see is that successive generations of students find their own voice and style, and by discovering confidence in their writing, discover confidence in themselves.

Our teaching challenge is to get students to think in sophisticated terms while they write on subjects generated by the reading assignments. Let me say at the outset that I believe in directed discussions focused on the material we read and the papers we write. I think of myself as an orchestra conductor trying to get the most out of each player and working with each individual to bring out his talent. If a student finds a mentor or two in his college career, that student will usually have a better experience, and we faculty teaching freshman seminars need be accessible to fill that role. No one is the appropriate mentor for everyone or the best kind of teacher for everyone, and good teaching comes in many modes.

Let me turn to a question I am often asked: "How have the changes in our discipline changed your teaching?" As I always have, I try to be a pluralist and introduce a number of possibilities for reading a text into a discussion, although the possibilities change in relation to the students we teach and the world we live in. I stepped on the tails of the dinosaurs when I arrived at Cornell in 1968, and some of my ideas may come from a period when—at least in the memories of some—a handful of larger-than-life creatures ruled the academic earth of my department and college. However, I like to think that I have a sensitivity to women and a multicultural environment that perhaps was not required in that era. Certainly our student body has evolved into a much richer and more varied group where *difference* is more respected.

My pedagogical goals are:

1.   To teach my students to write lucidly and logically and to teach them to make an argument that both uses the examples of close reading to support concepts *and* uses historical and cultural contexts. (My mantra: "Always the text; Always historicize.")

2.   To encourage my students to think independently and challenge accepted truths when they think them wrong or in need of modification.

3.   To teach my students how to compare, contrast, and synthesize; while I use 270 course materials as a paradigm, these skills are transferable to other courses and inquiries beyond our particular subject matter. We need to teach our students to use these skills in responding

79

to the texts they are reading, not only in the obligatory way that we require in "conclusions" to essays, but throughout their essays' arguments as well as in their thinking of the body of material that constitutes a course. This emphasis on comparison and synthesis has the added benefit of making them think of the course as a coherent body of material rather than an arbitrary sequence of unrelated material generated by the teacher's preferences. Too often the reading in freshman writing courses takes place in a vacuum without sufficient explanation about the *logic* of the syllabi.

4.   To teach them to read closely and well, alert to nuances in language, and to see the value of reading in a visual age. I continue to teach close reading because that is what I believe teaches attentiveness to language in writing and in speech.

5.   To stress the need to articulate ideas orally. When we get an intimation of what seems true or right by examining evidence and developing reasoned arguments, we should want to express it for others and ourselves, not in a spirit of shouting down or dismissiveness but in the spirit of participating in a community.

6.   To demonstrate that when we attend to what others are saying and writing, we are learning and that when we argue about meaning (as Plato knew), we come to understand how we know what we know.

We as teachers need to develop in our students skills that are transferable to other disciplines but also to future careers as well as to their thoughtful participation in community activities. We need to place less emphasis on pre-professional skills for putative English professors and more on skills that will make our students productive citizens who might participate in civic life, including service on library and museum boards or school boards.

III. The Freshman Seminar as an Introduction to University Intellectual Opportunities

I like to think of the subtitle of my 270 class as *Cornell Optics*. I continue to think of my class as a process of opening doors and windows.

I believe every freshman section of the writing program should in part be a course in opening eyes and helping the students see more. I call attention on a regular basis both on my email list and in class to the vast variety of concerts, lectures, films, writing opportunities for newspapers and magazines that make *Cornell* Cornell. In a sense, we are like Henry Fielding's Host in *Tom Jones*. In my teaching I encourage the students to partake and participate.

In all my courses, I also utilize the resources on campus: the art museum as well as, more informally, the plays performed at the Cornell theater, films shown on campus, and the architecture and design of our campus. I take as my guests any 270 students who wish to attend the three major Cornell theater plays performed during the semester that they are in my course and often offer them theater tickets after they finish the course.

During the first 75-minute class we look out the window for the final half hour and discuss some of the buildings and how they reflect diverse styles and tastes, depending on when they were built and what their purpose is. Then we move to the other side of the window and see that many of our conclusions need be amended when we look from a different angle, and see different facades of the same buildings and also see the same buildings in slightly different settings.

I meet at least one class session in the Johnson Art Museum and generate an assignment in which I ask the class to compare fiction with paintings or sculptures. Before that class I ask each student to select a work that he or she will discuss. The class at the art museum emphasizes the distinction between the spatiality of the visual and the temporality of literary arts, while also showing students that, contrary to what many have thought, painting and sculpture may have a narrative element and literature may have spatial organization.

IV. Teaching Writing

Let me return to another of Orwell's assertions from the same splendid essay:

> The mixture of vagueness and sheer incompetence is the most marked characteristic of modern English prose, and especially of any kind of

political writing. As soon as certain topics are raised, the concrete melts into the abstract and no one seems able to think of turns of speech that are not hackneyed; prose consists less and less of words chosen for the sake of their meaning, and more and more of phrases tacked together like sections of a prefabricated hen-house. (Orwell 1954, 71)

To avoid the kind of language Orwell indicts, our goals as writing teachers must be to teach precision of thought, clarity of expression, logic of argument, and individuality—and, yes sometimes, controlled passion—of voice.

My first class is necessarily mostly organizational and introductory; I explain the logic of the syllabus and course policies and procedures. I might add that for freshmen to understand that a writing course has a coherent perspective, the teacher must explain what he or she is doing on a regular basis and particularly *why* they are reading the works they are reading. It is most troubling to me that when I teach English 270 in the second semester, many of my students—as well as any freshman advisees I might have—often do not remember the title of their first-term freshman writing courses or what their teacher's name is.

As a writing teacher I stress sentence variety. On each essay I stipulate three or so sentence types that must be included and underlined such as a "Not only […] but also," an "If […] then" sentence, a rhetorical question, a subjunctive contrary to fact, a sentence beginning with a gerund, a sentence beginning with a modifying present participle, a sentence beginning with a noun clause. I ask each student to mark these sentences with a colored pen. I also stress the desirability of substituting strong verbs for "There are," "There is," and "It is."

Because students are often on the frontier of their understanding when dealing with complex texts such as *Notes from Underground*, they tend to write convoluted sentences. Indeed, reading such texts as *Notes from Underground* and *Death in Venice* may, I fear, encourage circumlocutious sentences. I emphasize that short, lucid sentences have their place. I also stress strong, conceptual topic sentences, a taut evolving argument, and the ability to integrate a specific story—or experience or piece of knowledge—with other stories and knowledge.

I should make clear that I teach two 75-minute classes a week, and that the classes meet Tuesday and Thursday. I begin each term with short essays that increase in length as the term progresses. I assign seven papers per term and, after the first one or two essays, I give the students a good deal of choice in my assignments. For one assignment, I also give students the option of writing a short story so they can see how to handle point of view, characterization, plot development, and beginnings and endings. Most take this option.

Graded papers are always handed back to the class after they are received, and I do this even in my larger classes where I am assisted by a graduate teaching assistant or graduate reader. While discussing the literary works, I not only emphasize the issues I want discussed in the papers, but demonstrate how a paper on the assignment or—if I give a choice among topics—assignments might be structured. Sometimes I assign papers asking students to discuss texts that we have not yet covered in class time in terms of issues and concepts that we have fore-grounded in the texts that we have been addressing in class. Other times I ask them to build on issues within a text that we have been examining in class, particularly when we are addressing complex texts, such as *Notes from Underground*, which they need to revisit to understand.

The first essay is due the third class. In the first few weeks when the students are not overwhelmed by other work, I assign shorter papers with shorter intervals between assignment and due date. I assign longer essays the Tuesday I return them and give the students nine days' writing time to the following Thursday. During the nine days between assignment and due date, I discuss in class how they might proceed on the assignments, and correspond on email with those seeking input on outlines and drafts. After returning their first assignment, we discuss their writing and discuss how papers might begin and end, how they should make an argument, and how to use evidence. By drawing upon their own writing experience, the class begins to work together. We work together to examine how to use evidence from the text, and how to structure a paragraph that moves sequentially from concept, to a middle level of discourse that negotiates between concept and specific, to specific evidence including perhaps a quotation, to precise comment in terms of the argument, to perhaps more evidence and comment, and then back to middle level of discourse, and finally back to concept.

On each subsequent day that I return papers, I discuss writing and address specific issues raised by the papers. Usually, after the first paper or so, while I may mention a number of issues, the focus is on one or two problems such as conceptual topic sentences or the need for more active voice or the way to organize evidence in making an argument or suggestions for sentence variety.

When reading a passage from a student paper or distributing copies of that paper for discussion, I have over the years alternated between anonymity and identifying the author. I discuss this issue early in the term and ask the class which they prefer. Within a class of 17—the maximum size for a Cornell freshman writing seminar— where the students come to know and respect one another, usually the student whose essay is being discussed identifies herself or himself. I think if one establishes a community of inquiry and is positive, and begins by commending the achievements of the essay under discussion, one can, with some exceptions, publicly identify students. However when a paper is substandard or if the student is doing work not up to the level of the class, I do not identify the student. If the student requests anonymity when the issue is raised at the beginning of term, then the student will not be identified.

My goal is to let each student find his or her own voice rather than homogenize their voices into one Proper Compositional Style. While I do not require it, I suggest keeping a loose-leaf journal, alternating days of writing about personal life with days writing about political and campus issues—or whatever is of interest to the student. I offer to read the non-personal pages during and/or after the course is over. Interestingly a number of students have taken up this suggestion after the course—and after the demands on their freshman first or second term have lessened—and brought me their journals to read.

On occasion, after collecting the papers on the due date, I immediately pass out the student papers to class members. Since I initiate this exercise after the first two assigned papers, I am able to select for each student reader a paper which either speaks to writing problems present in the student reader's own work or a paper which provides an example of how to address successfully one or two of the student reader's major problems. (Of course one cannot always anticipate what will be handed in, but after two sets, one becomes a good guesser.) I give the student graders about half an hour to make comments; sometimes I ask for a letter grade, too.

Although we might do this exercise in which students read other students' essays twice, no one grades the same student more than once. When reading the papers, I observe how the student grader has responded not so much to evaluate the grader but to learn what the grader sees and understands when reading the work of others. Normally, since the students are in large part learning the grading standards from me, the students' grades are about the same as mine. Often I have asked the student graders for comments without grades but since we are in a grade-oriented era, perhaps the evaluation with a grade has more bite.

Of course I regrade all the essays and provide substantive typed comments as well as handwritten marginal comments. My typed comments not only give an overview of the paper's strengths and problems but also refer to specific passages within the paper. Over the years my emphasis has switched to the typed final comments— although I make comments within, too—in part because my English 270 students do not make a plethora of technical errors. Years ago I experimented with dispensing with paper grades in favor of only comments, waiting to give a final grade when I received students' final folders containing all their work. But, because the students began to ask me what grade they would have received had they received a grade, I have the last 15 years returned to letter grades after the first paper or two.

Each of us has our own idiosyncrasies as writing teachers. More than once a term, I acknowledge—as I think we all should—that faculty have diverse ideas about writing essays and that while we can all agree on grammar, punctuation, and spelling, not everyone agrees on the use of active voice or the use of the first person. (I do not mind occasional first-person intrusion.) Indeed, I teach in the spirit of "This is true, isn't it?" and try to eschew the dogmatism about writing to which my generation and some of our students have been exposed. We need remember that the House of Good Writing has many rooms.

My 270 students make few grammatical errors. On occasion they use comma splices or use semi-colons to separate an independent clause from a dependent clause. When my students are unaware of the terminology and rules of grammar, I refer them to the Harbrace College Handbook. I am often asked whether students have changed over the past 40 years. In general the answer is, "Not much—except on occasion recent students may not have been taught grammatical terms; thus I have to explain what an independent clause or passive voice is."

While acknowledging that scientific writing has different requirements and explaining why this is so, I stress the need for active voice in all my courses because I want students to be aware of how creative and polemical authors make decisions which affect readers' responses. This stress on active voice helps me to teach students the difference between authorial and resistant readings. I want them to use active voice to describe the author's creative decisions and the narrator's self-dramatization. Even in class discussion I insist that students use more accurate terminology to describe what is going on within a text than "it says" or "they say".

I do what I call *needs-based assignments*—that is, assignments based on the students' progress. Some students might continue to write shorter essays; some might revise more essays than others; some might propose topics that are a little outside the rubric of papers for an assignment. In addition to one stipulated revision assignment, each student may revise as often as she or he wishes. The original grade is not erased, but the second and subsequent grades are recorded. I give the first paper or two "S" or "U" although usually the weaker few get an "S-". Rather than indicate one grade for form and another for content, split grades ("S/S-" or "A-/B+") indicate my unwillingness—some might say, inability—to make broad distinctions.

Usually I have two office conferences per term with each student, but if an occasional student does not schedule a second one after continued invitations, I won't chase her or him around. However, some students want to discuss every paper and that is fine. I also remain after class for informal discussions which are often as valuable as formal conferences.

V. Teaching Reading

My interest in narratology and in modern art informs my teaching as it does my writing. While I take cognizance of recent theory, in my teaching and writing I still find value in an Aristotelian perspective that stresses the Doesness of a text and insists on the inextricable relationship between the aesthetic and ethical. Such a perspective asks how texts shape readers, what conscious and unconscious decisions an author makes to create a structure of effects, and what kind of form and genre the author chooses. I discuss the difference between Aristotelian approaches, which argue that the text generates effects, and reader-response criticism, which stresses what the reader brings to the text. I suggest a transactional theory of reading that takes account of the differences between authorial and resistant readings.

In my classes, I explain the place of resistant-reading perspectives— perspectives that *resist* the point of view that an author (or painter) thought he was expressing and built into his text. Often these resistant readings have contributed rich feminist, gay, ecological, minority, and other multicultural perspectives that the author ignored. With these approaches came changes in how we discuss reading assignments and the writing topics we assign. For example, discussion of the homoerotic implications of male bonding plays a larger role in my discussion of *The Secret Sharer* than it once did. Thus the canon changes even if the names of the texts are the same.

My teaching has always been closely related to my scholarship. If one believes as I do that the best readings are those that explain the phenomena within a text, one tests one's readings in a classroom. But, depending both on how we change and how our historical and cultural context change, "best reading" is an evolving concept that varies from one reading to the next. My experience teaching texts finds its way into my writings, from my books on Conrad and Joyce's *Ulysses* to the chapter in *The Case for a Humanistic Poetics* entitled "The Ethics of Reading" which uses "Araby" as a paradigm. Indeed, my decades of teaching *The Dead* and *The Secret Sharer* certainly influenced my writing the biographical and historical introductions, the critical over-views, and the psychoanalytic essays for my editions of those texts in Bedford's Case Studies in Contemporary Criticism series.

Without using much of the jargon of contemporary criticism, I differentiate in one semi-lecture class between different traditional and more recent critical approaches and define deconstructive, Marxist, New Historical, cultural studies, and, especially, feminist approaches. (Remember that I am mostly teaching students who have been to the best private and public schools and have been exposed to teachers who have trained at top universities.) When we discuss texts I try to make the students aware of what approaches we are using. Thus when we do the full-length Woolf novel, *To the Lighthouse*, for two weeks, I particularly focus on writing and reading as a woman and what that gender difference means. Of course, gender issues play a larger role in most of the discussions than they once did. One choice for the final assignment is a feminist reading of *To the Lighthouse*.

VI. Building the Bridge between Reading and Writing

I believe that close reading of complex creative texts teaches that style enacts values, that the expectations of audiences change, and that *every choice* a writer makes affects how an audience reads his or her text. I discuss the first stories in terms of formal issues of point of view and show how they reveal the world in which the speaker lives. Because these texts address problems of unreliable and imperceptive narrators, we discuss degrees of reliability and perceptivity. Later I move on to third-person omniscient narrators. I stress voice and persona as a way of getting students to be aware of how, when writing their own essays, structure and choice of language enact their voice and persona.

As the syllabus of English 270 progresses, the focus continues on ways of telling but includes such issues as *doppelgängers* (*The Secret Sharer,* "The Prussian Officer," Joyce's "Counterparts," *Notes from Underground,* and *Death in Venice*); the difference between character and characterization; how setting functions to reinforce theme and structure within an imagined ontology (Faulkner's "Dry September," and *The Dead*); the difference between story and discourse; the differences between, on the one hand, the realism of such writers as Hemingway, Joyce, Conrad, and, on the other, stories that depend on fantasy and parable such as Lawrence's "The Rocking Horse Winner," Kipling's "The Gardener," and Kafka's "The Hunter Gracchus" and *Metamorphosis*. In one informal unit, we discuss the implications of how stories and novels begin and end. Of course the more complex texts need be discussed in terms of most of the aforementioned distinctions rather than merely one of them.

After the first class discussion devoted to a discussion of how the point of view of the slightly older retrospective teller functions in Joyce's "Araby," I might ask the class to discuss in their first assigned essay how the speaker is a self-dramatizing character in Hemingway's "Another Country." In my class on "Araby" I show how formal problems of point of view are inextricably related to historical issues such as Joyce's views of the effects of a stifling Catholic education and of the dominance of the British in Ireland upon the boy's perceptions. My stress in the early classes is that the narrator's words reveal as they conceal and conceal as they reveal. The first essay, perhaps a page and half to two pages, assigned after the second class (but after the first discussion of the reading) also has, among other goals, the purpose of seeing if there are students who do not belong in the 200-level class, but instead in a course that provides more remedial writing help.

VII. Creating a Community of Inquiry

At every level from freshman seminar to graduate seminar, I try to make my classes more than a site where I set assignments and the students do them to fulfill a course requirement. Needless to say this is a goal for which we always reach and we often fall short. But I should like to suggest how we might develop a community of inquiry where each student understands learning as a process, takes responsibility for being prepared each day, takes his assignments seriously, feels himself part of a functioning group, and writes his assignments with a sense of pride in his work and his evolving writing voice.

When we do a short reading assignment, I ask about half the class to prepare a specific subject for discussion; when I do a novella or the one longer novel, I might ask the entire class to prepare a subject. Thus for "Araby," two students might speak about the retrospective telling, another the beginning, another the end, someone else the theme of Catholicism, another student the theme of empire, two others might be asked to think of the issue of guilt and how it shapes the retrospective teller, another would focus on the role of women, yet another the speaker's prepubescent psychosexuality. When two students are assigned the same subject, I encourage them to talk to one another and work together. The students are resources for the assigned subjects when they arise; if, as occasionally occurs, the students are not called on to give a minute or two presentation, they almost always raise their hands and participate. On other occasions, I assign a small group of three or four—and ask one to be the coordinator—to present a text to the class for 10 or 15 minutes.

My goal is to have every student comment in some way in at least two classes out of three. Once students begin to participate they rarely stop. When they participate (rather than sit in the bleachers and watch), they feel better about themselves and the class. The class becomes the student's own experience, not something she or he observes as a bystander. More importantly, when a student articulates ideas, the student often clarifies those ideas for himself, and that clarification continues when listening to ensuing responses to his or her contribution.

Email has changed teaching, opening up new ways of bridging the gap between the dorm room and the classroom and of creating an exciting nexus between the two sites. On the first day I collect email addresses and establish an email list; each student is expected to make three substantive contributions to the discussion of course texts or recurring issues; most contribute more often. Indeed, as the term progresses and the students become better readers, the colloquies on email are often stunning not only in their thoughtfulness and sophistication but in the precision, lucidity, and energy of their writing. At the end of the term, along with their essays, the students submit their email contribution in their folders.

I encourage both email comments addressed to the entire class and individual dialogues with me. Freshmen—and except for a very occasional transfer or student who has postponed a writing seminar, my 270 students are freshmen—look to their teachers in small classes more than they do to their formal advisors. We teachers need make clear that we are accessible to them in office hours and open to email and phone inquiries. I answer email several times a day from home, and I am also accessible by phone from 8am–10pm. Of course the students write each other "off list," and that is exactly what I want. I have no problem with a student showing a draft to a friend or roommate or other class member as long as the student writes his own paper. But the email has another important function in building a community of inquiry. Students are also encouraged to share with the class information about concerts, plays, or sporting events in which they participate; as a result students attend one another's activities and build commitment to our community.

One way that a class becomes a community of inquiry is regular and prompt attendance, even for classes beginning at 8.40am. We need have rules for attendance and make a show of knowing who is present. Usually in English 270 I have over the entire term less than one absence per student, and more than half the students do not miss a class. I usually arrive early and, as the class assembles, I ask what films they have seen and share my views of films I have seen; at other times we might discuss Cornell theater plays or campus issues, or adult choices with which freshmen are faced such as whether to join a fraternity or sorority and how to organize their time among the demands of schoolwork, activities, and part-time jobs.

In these pre-class discussions which, on occasion, overflow into the first few minutes of our 75-minute class period, I might mention such freshman anxieties as what resources are available if they are in trouble in a course as well as how to address difficulties with study habits or time management, particularly at hectic times before midterms and finals. At the end of each month a few students and/or I bring a little food for a brief class party, and, while nibbling for 15 minutes, we discuss films, course issues, Cornell issues, or even national issues. I take the class to dinner the last week.

At the end of term I give students an informal reading list, suggesting further reading in authors we have read as well as authors we have not read, especially authors related to those we have read. I offer to read their work in the future. I remind them that when they read they should always be aware of the way a piece is written. For examples of good (but not always faultless) writing, I suggest that they should continue to read the editorial page and the Op-Ed page in the *New York Times* and perhaps *The New Yorker*. We have an informal class reunion—often a pizza dinner—the next semester, and sometimes these reunions continue for four years. Since the email lists remain through their graduation, I and class members continue to write one another after the class is over. Many of the 270 students take other classes from me, some become my major advisees, and quite often we keep in touch not only in the years after graduation but for decades.

What, finally, is a community of inquiry? It is a class in which students commit themselves not merely to the teacher, but to the material and each other in a spirit of learning. In a community of inquiry the class does not stop when students and teachers separate and the course ends. The students speak to one another outside the classroom and on email about their reading and writing, and carry their intellectual relationships beyond the life of the course.

Especially in the humanities, we need to stress learning as an end itself and as a lifelong odyssey so that our students, as Constantine Cavafy put it in the previously quoted poem "Ithaka:"

> Keep Ithaka always in mind.
> Arriving there is what you're destined for.
> […]
> Ithaka gave you the marvelous journey

Without her you wouldn't have set out
[…]
Wise as you will have become, so full of experience,
you'll have understood by then what these Ithakas mean.

The students need understand that Cornell—and life—is composed of many Ithacas and that these Ithacas represent the wonder of learning.

4

Eating Kosher Ivy: Jews as Literary Intellectuals

In this chapter I shall consider the place of the Jewish literary intellectual, the diaspora of Jewish public intellectuals from New York urban culture to the American universities, and the consequent transformation of public intellectuals into literary intellectuals. Writing from a personal perspective and suspecting that some of my memories—like the memories of all of us—are distorted by time and by the demands of narrative teleology that require a coherent story, I write about my own diaspora—my own career odyssey—from a suburban enclave into the world of literary scholars.

I. Situating Myself

In the 1940s and early 1950s when I was growing up in Rockville Centre, a Long Island suburban community that was one-third Jewish, the Holocaust was a repressed subject among Jews who were often quite assimilated but, with the long shadow cast by events in Europe, wary of the gentile world—sometimes even more so than their parents. I had my Bar Mitzvah in a synagogue, which was the first temple in Rockville Centre, one my maternal grandparents were instrumental in establishing. I remember that much was made of my maternal grandfather and grandmother not only as Jewish elders but also as community elders, for they also played a role in secular affairs before moving back to Manhattan after the war. My grandfather did not know a word of Hebrew or Yiddish and, like all my grandparents, was born in the United States. If my memory is correct, the Holocaust was barely mentioned in the Conservative religious school I attended three times a week until my Bar Mitzvah at age 13.

Why was the Holocaust a suppressed subject? Did assimilated American Jews feel they had something to be ashamed of because they did not prevent the destruction of their European counterparts? Did they fear provoking American anti-Semitism by special pleading? Was it that my parents' generation thought that children's sensibilities could not deal with the horrors of genocide?

Jewish silence during and after the war mirrored the much more striking silence, ineffectuality, and complicity of the entire American community that, despite the Nuremberg trials and the gruesome pictures in *Life Magazine* and newsreels, chose to repress how they were helpless onlookers or even tacit if unwilling accomplices. We now know how much the American political leadership knew and how little they did about it. The atrocities committed on blacks in these years, particularly in the South, rightfully focused attention on civil rights, but there was surprising little linkage to the wartime persecution of Jews, notwithstanding the prominence of Jews in the civil rights movement in the 1950s and 1960s.

My mother's family was quite comfortable. They had moved to Long Island in the early years of the twentieth century. My father's family, once reasonably comfortable in the luggage business, got by after the Depression. They moved to Rockville Centre to open a dry-cleaning business, one of many not very successful enterprises, and my mother's parents met them as their customers. My father was (I suspect, barely) acceptable as an eligible Jewish male. Awkward family pictures show my mother's parents and my father's mother—my father's father died before I was born—looking as if the two families belonged to different worlds. Bar-Mitzvahed but not really educated in Jewish religious practices, my father became a Certified Public Accountant, a temple member, and did reasonably well economically, but never had the elegance of my mother's parents. Until he died at almost 91, he was a frugal and prudent man.

Both of my grandfathers were German Jews. One grandmother, who was born in St. Louis in 1888, was a Polish Jew, but her family, like those of all my grandparents, immigrated to the USA at a time close to the Civil War. My mother's mother descended from Hungarian Jews. As I am reminded when I visit Vienna and Budapest, some of my mother's cooking reflects her Austrian-Hungarian heritage. Some years ago I saw photographs of my mother's forebears that were never before shown to me. They were German Jews born as far back as 1800, including at least one in a German military uniform. They were my relatives, many of whom must have been left behind and whose children or children's children probably died in the Holocaust. In fact, I learned from the Yad Vashem Holocaust database that Jews from Essen—the place from which our Schwarz family originated with what is for Jews the unusual spelling of our name—died in the Holocaust.

My maternal grandfather was a formal man. Until I was 10, I thought he took a shower with his tie on. My father's father, born in the United States, insisted that his children learn German. My father spoke of an uncle who sympathized with the Germans during World War I. I always imagine how German these people must have felt even here. What an irony!

While I had some sense of Jewish identity, my childhood and adolescence were insulated from flagrant anti-Semitism and my friends were just as likely, if not more likely, to be non-Jewish as Jewish. I confronted my Jewish identity when, in 1961–1962, I did my junior year of college in what was still post-war Europe. I saw the Anne Frank house, was approached by Jews with numbers on their arms who wanted to meet American Jews, and I saw the shards of the Warsaw ghetto. As I drove through Germany a number of times, I slept in inexpensive small guesthouses only to awaken and see pictures of SS officers on the walls.

I married a woman who converted to Judaism; we were married by the Reform Jewish Rabbi who presided over the process and ceremony of conversion. My sons had their Bar Mitzvahs in a Conservative Temple, the only temple in Ithaca until recently, and I still am a dues-paying member of the congregation. I married again, this time to a Jewish woman, and the ceremony was held in that synagogue. Of the small number of Jews in my English Department at Cornell, I am the only member of the local temple, although I only go to services on the High Holy Days and never for more than part of the long Conservative services.

I remain an agnostic, but with deep spiritual—if I may I use that term—ties to my Jewish heritage. Passover and Hanukkah mean a great deal as family holidays, and my wife and I light the candles on Friday night if we are home—if we remember. My visit to Israel in 1985–1986, built around a lecture at Hebrew University in Jerusalem, accentuated my moderate Zionist sympathies. More and more, when I travel in Europe, I visit synagogues and Jewish sites, and learn about Jewish history.

I have become more interested in my Jewish heritage as I became aware of how my Jewishness defines me as a scholar. The development of identity studies which began with feminism and later Afro-American studies enabled Jewish scholars to examine their own heritage and history within the borders of academia. Had I written my book on Holocaust narratives entitled *Imagining the Holocaust* in the early 1970s when I was trying to make tenure, it would have been a passport to obscurity.

II. The Jew as (Not Always Comfortable) Guest in the House of English Literature

Many of the teachers who most influenced me were, by the standards of the day, outsiders and oddities: the first black teacher in my Long Island school district passionately taught me ninth- and eleventh-grade English. Barbara Lewalski, the only woman in the 1963–1968 period in the English Department at Brown, where I did my graduate work, was one of my paradigmatic figures. In college, two closeted gay professors influenced my thinking at a time when lifelong bachelors were suspect, and one of them became an enduring influence and friend.

One found no tenured Jews on the rolls of Ivy League English departments before World War II; indeed there were not many Irish and Italians either. In part because of the importance of Albert Einstein and in part because of the involvement of Jews in the Manhattan

Project, Jews were welcome in the more egalitarian and meritocratic world of the hard sciences before they were welcomed in the more elitist world of the humanities. Jews did make inroads in English departments of public universities before they were welcomed in the Ivy League. For example, the University of California at Berkeley had a considerable number of Jews on its English faculty by the late 1960s, the time when I began my teaching career at Cornell.

Jewish graduate students were expected to pursue the authorized subjects, to submerge their identity, and to find a common pursuit with other graduate students in studying Anglo-Catholic and Puritan writers. Raised in a Jewish home in New York, one distinguished female academic told me that she wrote on Flannery O'Connor at Berkeley, and "identified," as she puts it, with O'Connor's Southern Catholicism, rather than with her own marginal situation as a Jew in a gentile universe.

As a graduate student at Brown, I did my share of cultural cross-dressing when writing my master's thesis on Christian imagery in Robert Browning's *The Ring and the Book* or working on a seminar paper on Edmund Spenser's *Shepherdes Calendar*. The department chair and a few of the faculty were Jews.

We need remember that the then dominant ideology, the New Criticism, not only sought to eliminate the biography of the author but to focus on the ideal reader. Such a focus not only homogenized the ethnic differences among the audience, but also assumed that all readers brought similar experience—a keen sensibility and know-ledge of literary tradition—to a text. The New Criticism and the other major Anglo-American formalism, Neo-Aristotelian criticism, emphasized aesthetic values at the expense of representation of an anterior world. Erich Auerbach's influential study *Mimesis* discussed representation as a formal matter, not one involving messy social issues. Written after he escaped from Nazi Germany, the book never situates the author as a Jew.

Major English departments in the 1960s and 1970s were domi-nated by Anglophiles. With few exceptions the anti-Semitic ravings of Pound—some of which found their way into his poetry—as well as the equally objectionable if less strident version of anti-Semitism in

Eliot's work, were either excused as the eccentricities of men of genius or dismissed as unsuitable matters of discussion. In "Circumscriptions: Assimilating T.S. Eliot's Sweeneys" in *People of the Book*, Rachel DuPlessis compellingly asks: "Were New Criticism and our carefully received reading strategies in some way complicit with the ravishing loss of Jewish particularity?" (Rubin-Dorsky and Fishkin 1996, 135–52, 139). In graduate school many of us, trained on the formalist rubric of organic form, read without noticing or pretended not to notice anti-Semitic passages. (While my dissertation director, Mark Spilka, was a Jew with ambiguous feelings about his Jewishness, he was one of the few who were cognizant of the anti-Semitism in these paradigmatic modern writers.) After all, were we not part of that imaginary audience of ideal readers on which New Criticism and Aristotelian criticism depended—even as we ignored the fact that the imagined audience of ideal readers were WASPs? We immersed ourselves in elaborate and arcane Christian theological debate to understand Milton or Hawthorne without reflecting that we were part of a different tradition, but perhaps we took secret satisfaction in learning that Milton knew Hebrew. Perhaps, too, we took pleasure in knowing that the exegetical tradition of literary criticism resembled the conversational and inquisitive mode of Talmudic studies, or what we—as assimilated Jews—imagined Talmudic study to be.

Figures such as M.H. Abrams, Harry Levin, Lionel Trilling—those who found a place within the Ivy League—as well as Irving Howe and Alfred Kazin—New York intellectuals who made their mark—became spiritual fathers to those of us who took up English and American Studies in the 1960s.[1] To that I would add Meyer Shapiro, the great Columbia art historian. Kazin and Howe embraced their Jewishness far more dramatically than my friend who called himself Mike Abrams and wrote under the name M.H. Abrams rather than use his actual name Meyer. Abrams eschewed being too Jewish, and rarely—at least in my presence—talked about his Jewishness until after he retired. Quietly he contributed generously to the United Jewish Appeal (UJA), but he created an identity as the archetypal Harvard-educated English professor: art connoisseur, pipe-smoking gourmet, lover of classical music, and dilettante, recorder-playing, dedicated Cornell sports fan. In conversation, he eschewed unpleasant topics from the shortcomings of colleagues to the Holocaust.

When I arrived at Cornell in 1968 I encountered in the English department a few older Jewish colleagues. Wary of being too Jewish, most had experienced anti-Semitism which they spoke of to younger Jewish scholars only after they knew them well and even then in hush-hush tones. My generation, too, was taught that it was best not to be too Jewish; as another colleague who moved to Cornell from Harvard put it, "As a graduate student, I was taught not to walk around with a Hebrew National Salami hanging out of my pocket." Some disguised their Jewish heritage by name changes or a refusal to acknowledge their Jewish ancestry. Virtually none of my Jewish colleagues had temple affiliations; some gave almost surreptitiously to the UJA, while others of Jewish parentage denied their Jewish heritage. One colleague, whose father had been at CCNY (The City College of New York) with my father and came from a distinguished Jewish family, not only denied his heritage but also responded tartly to a UJA solicitation, "You mustn't assume from my name that I have Jewish origins."

I confess to having always felt uncomfortable within the mostly WASPish world of Ivy League English departments. My New York brashness was at odds with some of the WASPish reticence. Except for my first two years, I have dealt mostly with non-Jewish chairs, at least some of whom seemed to be uncomfortable dealing with Jews. The only exception was one woman who, while far more aggressive than I in pursuing her agenda, not only very much played down her Jewish identity but ran the department for some people at the expense of others.

Was it my own discomfort that drew me to outsiders for my subjects? For my college honors theses and PhD dissertation I chose as my subject Joseph Conrad, a Polish émigré who felt himself an outsider in England. For my first book, I chose Benjamin Disraeli, the Jew who became Prime Minister and always—even though he had been converted as a boy, thanks to his father—thought of himself as a Jew and maintained a strong if eccentric sense of Jewish identity. After writing two literary studies on Conrad, I turned to James Joyce, who left his homeland dominated by the Catholic Church and the British Crown to live in exile, and who identified with Jews. Teaching and writing on Joyce required knowledge of what to me were exotic Catholic rituals and legends, but I did focus a good deal in my *Reading Joyce's "Ulysses"* on Leopold Bloom as a Jew.

The dominant style for Jews in my department has been to mimic WASPish customs and behavior. The person who was chair during most of my assistant professor years had a preferred way of saying "No" that at first sounded like "Yes." He would say "I agree with you on principle," before explaining, sometimes two conversations or weeks later, why he couldn't or wouldn't do something. To my ethnic heritage, with its emphasis on frankly confronting opposing views, this mode of discourse seemed incredibly odd. Even though I had done my graduate work at Brown—where Jews in the English department did not hide their Jewishness quite as much as at Cornell—I was not familiar with the professional indirection in the form of litotes and euphemism.

Certainly it was made clear to me that my New York accent and direct if not brash manner were odd. That I didn't go to Harvard for any of my degrees was another minus in some eyes in a department which, until 2002, had Harvard PhDs as department chairs for 25 years. I made a point of being who I was and not pretending I was someone else. I spoke my mind at meetings, disagreed when I thought it was a matter of principle to do so, and probably didn't always do myself good in the process.

Among the Jews I have known at Cornell, what it is like to be a Jew and teach English and American literature has never been, so far as I know, the subject of a public or private discussion in my forty years here. And yet for those of us who are Jewish, and our students, it is surely a more compelling subject than so many that we address. Why do Jews act as if this issue didn't matter? Even in *People of the Book: Thirty Scholars Reflect on Their Jewish Identity* (Rubin-Dorsky and Fishkin 1996), one finds a fair amount of evasion of what makes literary studies appealing to Jews, what defines the Jewish contribution, and how Jews relate to multicultural colleagues. Why do contemporary Jews in literature departments—much like the first group of Jews who were on these faculties—often accept without resistance being grouped by minorities as part of a Caucasian hegemony when their experience has much in common with those very minorities? Indeed, it is curious how—perhaps as the social price for acceptance—Jewish scholars in English departments only pushed for Jewish studies after the establishment of other ethnic and minority studies.

Have I experienced covert or overt anti-Semitism in my professional career? I could cite scattered anecdotes, but the truth is I don't know. For example, I was at a party in 1973 after the Arab–Israeli conflict that year when I overheard a senior and esteemed member of my department declaiming to his listeners, "The Jews on campus get uppity whenever Israel batters the Arabs." Yet I did get tenure at a time and in a department when many colleagues didn't. Certainly in recent years Cornell accolades and titles have come to me, and I feel grateful every day for the opportunities I have had.

III. Leslie Fiedler's Challenge to the New Criticism

In the 1960s every Jewish graduate student in literature knew the fairy tale of Leslie Fiedler who was exiled in Missoula, Montana, where he wrote and taught before returning to the East to SUNY Buffalo. In his life and work he thumbed his nose at the academic establishment and parochial historical criticism and what he saw as the narrow formalism of New Criticism, while making a very substantial reputation based primarily on one important and subversive 1960 book, *Love and Death in the American Novel*.

Published when he was in his 40s, Fiedler's book was embraced by younger academics and graduate students as relevant to overlooked themes and issues.

At a time when the relevance of literary study was being increasingly called into question by rampant McCarthyism and, later, the Vietnam War, the anti-war protest movement, and the resulting fissures between the university and society, Fiedler's book argued that literary study was central to our lives. Fiedler's bold discussion of psychosexual and political issues fulfilled the desire of younger academics for a more lively and engaged critical discourse. For Fiedler, literary criticism was, as he wrote in an encomium to his mentor, William Ellory Leonard,

> an act of total moral engagement, in which tact, patience, insolence, and piety consort strangely but satisfactorily together; nor can anyone who once listened to [Leonard] believe that the truth one tries to tell about literature is finally different from the truth one tries to tell about the indignities and rewards of being the kind of man one is—an American, let's say, in the second half of the twentieth century, learning to read his country's books. (Fiedler 1996, n.p.)

For American, some of us in the 1960s read Jew.

Retrospectively we can see that Fiedler enacts the ambiguity of Jews in English studies who, on the one hand, study a majority culture, accommodate to it, and are shaped by it, but, on the other, not only arrogate that culture for our own understanding and professional ends, but often bring to the subject an outsider's perspective and to the profession's customs and manners a somewhat different set of values. We make English studies our instrument, even as it makes us the instrument of English studies, its voice, and its spokespeople. Put another way: like other conquerors, we become the conquered.

In Fiedler's work on Joyce, we see not only his kinship with Leopold Bloom but feel he is writing about his own experience in the academy: "Anti-Semitism is everywhere in *Ulysses* the chief, almost the sole mode of relating to Jews available to gentiles; and indeed it is only in response to it that Bloom can feel himself a Jew at all, since ritually and ethnically he scarcely qualifies" (Fiedler, quoted in Kellman and Malin 1991, 55). Fiedler, like many Jews of his generation, writes as a Jew responding to a gentile world, which defines him as a Jew *and* as a representative of his people to outsiders.

IV. Finding a Home in a Restricted Neighborhood

How does being a secular Jew with an emphasis on this life in this world shape my sensibility? In answering that question, let us remember that each Jew has his own particular background and story to tell. Jewishness taught me that the fabric of everyday life matters more than one controlling ideology. That I am a humanistic critic who has insisted that literature is by humans, about humans and for humans is related to my concept of being Jewish. So, too, is my interest in the novel. It may be that being Jewish taught me that each reader, like each character in the novel, needs be taken seriously. For me each reader also means each student I teach.

Because Jews have historically lived on the margin—in ghettoes and shtetls, never sure of what pogroms tomorrow will bring—we have tended to be skeptical of sweeping universals and to dwell in particulars. Traditionally, Jews accept a world of fragments and enjoy small pleasures. The weekly routines focusing on the Sabbath and for religious Jews daily prayers in morning and evening paradoxically focus on the temporal dimension even while providing temporary escape from that dimension. Jewish theology is more concerned with relations between humans and God and between humans themselves than with a specific vision of the hereafter. Even Orthodox Jews stress the gap between man and God and hence turn their attention to the world in which they live.

For most Jews other than the ultra-orthodox, reading and interpreting biblical texts is an open and exegetical process. When one looks at the Talmud—a record of rabbinic discussions pertaining to Jewish law—one sees an unresolved dialogue among diverse commentators. In Judaism there are no *ex cathedra* statements, no Nicene creed, no attempt to resolve interpretive questions with single statement. In the Passover Haggadah the various rabbis comment dialogically upon the meaning of the Exodus story and specifically the meaning of the Passover customs, but the discussion is not resolved. The very term Haggadah means "the telling." The Haggadah is an open and evolving text that responds to changing historical circumstances. Before the founding of the State of Israel, it often took on a Zionist coloration to encourage the emigration of Eastern European Jews who were victims of pogroms and the Holocaust. The focus became more and more upon the captivity in Egypt as a metaphor not only for the diaspora in general but for state-sponsored pogroms, most notably what Lucy Davidowicz has called the War against the Jews or what we know as the Holocaust.

Thus the Talmudic exegetical tradition—a tradition of commentary—encouraged debate and dissent. I regard discussions of texts I teach and in particular professional literary criticism as a kind of continuing Midrash or commentary on literary texts. The tradition of studying the Torah and endlessly debating its meaning, of allowing dissent in its codification, gave space for specific and diverse readings that resisted universals, for elegant arguments for different positions, and for pluralism without dogmatism (the imposition of one position) or relativism (the notion that all views are equal).

Openness to diverse perspectives is not at odds with making choices and judgments or with understanding that in some situations we cannot give equal weight to all interests. Just as I reject measuring life on a vertical dimension which assumes that we are poised between heaven and hell and that this life is a prelude to another life, I am skeptical of readings of the texts in only one coordinate, whether Marxist, gay, feminist, or post-structural. All of the aforementioned are important ways of perceiving but need to be conceived as part of a pluralistic and dialogic epistemology.

Finally, my work has focused on ethical issues. Jews derived a strong sense of ethics from this Talmudic tradition of extracting from the Bible its moral implications and applicability for living today. Thus Jewish thinking derives much more from practice than theology. As Susanne Klingenstein writes:

> The absence of a single work outlining Jewish ethics, the moral theory behind ritual observance or orthopractice, has to do with the fact that ethical insights are regarded as an outgrowth of a specific discretionary form of behavior, which requires you to examine every act and action, to do nothing carelessly and thoughtlessly: Jewish moral thought emerged as a consequence of moral conduct. (Rubin-Dorsky and Fishkin 1996, 193)

Jewish tradition is ethically based—isn't the Talmud a discussion about law and ethics?—with an emphasis on what Aristotle called the "ineluctable modality of the visible" (and Joyce redefined into Stephen Dedalus's "What you damn well have to see"). Moreover, in Eastern Europe, the hereafter was often less a concern than eking out a living in the face often of arbitrary changes in the political winds. Unlike the Christian or Greek tradition, Jewish tradition eschewed universal explanations and sought to explore the human dilemma in a complex antagonistic world where Jews were marginalized, isolated, and persecuted. Jews by necessity lived in time and looked for partial solutions.

V. Jews as Public Intellectuals

Whether they acknowledge it or not, Jews are often guests in American and English traditions which have been driven by primary writings and criticism that were in turn driven by different religious and cultural assumptions. There is something paradoxical about Jews teaching texts written by believing Christians who think that the Jews are at best apostates and heretics and at worst Christ-murderers, and about Jews reading critics who did little to separate themselves from these views and who socially looked upon Jews from a steep and icy peak. At elite universities some Jews accommodated themselves to these traditions and even crossed-dressed as gentiles, and in my experience, all too few struggled to understand the aforementioned paradoxes. Those that did were, like Alfred Kazin and Irving Howe, more likely to teach in urban public universities such as the City University of New York (CUNY).

Except for Trilling and the art historian Shapiro at Columbia, the Jewish New York intellectuals were considered academic outsiders by many Ivy League Anglo-Saxon elitists in the 1950s and 1960s. Jewish figures such as Kazin, Howe, and Fiedler all worked mostly on American literature rather than the more validated English tradition. *Partisan Review* as well as *Commentary* helped establish the prominence of Saul Bellow, Bernard Malamud, and Philip Roth. Writing about second-generation Jews who became immersed in the tradition of Western culture, Terry A. Cooney observes:

106

What attracted a certain group of young intellectuals was a cultural promise, a literary tradition, and a pattern of social protest that together provided a basis for rejecting middle-class culture. [...] The sense of universal significance associated with their educational commitments seemed the opposite of the narrow concern young intellectuals saw in the Jewish community. (Cooney 1986, 14–15)

Jewish intellectuals existed on a kind of borderland between Jewish and gentile culture. Abandoning the security of their own communities without finding full acceptance in the communities of which they strove to be part, they became at once cosmopolitan and marginal. Within New York, with Jewish intellectuals like Irving Howe, Irving Kristol, and Norman Podhoretz, however, their Jewishness created a community which could not exist elsewhere, and a sense of belonging to an urban Jewish culture. Paradoxically, Jews within the New York intellectual community felt a common bond even while eschewing being too culturally Jewish.

While a shared sense of Jewishness formed a common bond among many of the contributors to *Partisan Review*, the plight of Jews in Europe was, somewhat surprisingly, not a focus of the magazine in the later 1930s and early 1940s. Trilling surely disassociated himself from self-conscious American-Jewish culture and denied its intellectual viability (see Cooney 1986, 237). The *Partisan Review* Jews preferred to see the Jew as rather cosmopolitan and also as marginal outsider, wanderer, and representative of the modern condition in that each American—and especially those not part of the WASP establishment—had to create his own cultural tradition. In what Cooney calls "resistance to anti-Semitism," the *Partisan Review* Jews embraced secularism, rationality, and the here-and-now world as an alternative to Christianity's mysticism and Platonism (Cooney 1986, 243).

What are public intellectuals? Knowledgeable in philosophy, history, public issues, and psychology, they are figures who speak to a wider audience than would a specialist and speak in lucid and comprehensible terms. They place their insights in a broad cultural context. Because of their wide intellectual experience, they earn the confidence of their readers and deserve their attention. They have gravitas.

Public intellectuals need an audience concerned with shared issues. In our diversified if not divided and divisive culture—where there is so much to be known and where special interest groups insist on focusing on their own issues—what matters to some is of no interest to others. I grew up in a world where a film by Truffaut or Fellini—or in New York a major exhibit at the Met on Picasso, Egypt, or China—needed to be seen and discussed as soon as possible. Now we are overwhelmed with information, books, films, and exhibits; while we always had to make choices, we now do so more often in terms of our cultural enclaves.

In the heyday of the *Partisan Review*, literary criticism was more accessible to a literate audience than it is now. In the humanities and social sciences, there has been a schism between academic culture and an intellectual audience. While the university world has become the center of intellectual activity, and we find Jews occupying prominent places as literary intellectuals at major universities, including the Ivy League, the retreat into private enclaves and jargon has been responsible for the decline of the literary critic as public intellectual.

VI. Conclusion: The Return of the Repressed

Let us think about how some Jewish literary intellectuals are now reclaiming the role of public intellectuals. For several decades, Jewish scholars passionately taught and still teach Anglo-American literature, but in recent years many have been rethinking whether these professional interests have repressed ethnic concerns. Why do assimilated Jewish scholars of different theoretical persuasions who used to discuss Wordsworth and Hardy in the halls now passionately discuss their Jewish pasts and their common interest in Holocaust studies even if they have different theoretical perspectives? How do we account for the return of the repressed and the sublimated? Is it in part because these Jews became tired of "cross-dressing" to gain acceptance in Anglophile English departments within prestigious universities?

For Jews in the literary departments the subject of the Holocaust may be one way to deal with the diaspora and indeed be a way of returning to our intellectual homeland. We have come a long way since Jews in American English departments were told that their Jewishness would be a negative factor in making their careers, or when non-Jews of lesser ability were encouraged to go into academia because they seemed to have the correct social graces.

When and why did cross-dressing abate for some Jews in prestigious English departments? For one thing, as I mentioned, ethnic studies made it permissible to own one's past; for another, cultural and ethnic studies expanded dramatically the range of what one could address in one's courses and research. In the wake of Afro-American, Asian-American, and Native American ethnic consciousness, it became permissible for Jews to discuss their past. That Jewish students wanted courses in their history was demonstrated by the numerical success of Holocaust courses and other Jewish studies courses. Often I have at least 50 students—many but not all with some Jewish forebears—who wanted to be members of my 15-member senior seminar on Holocaust memoirs and fiction.

As they reach mid-career and perhaps realizing that their professional lives have not so many years to go, many Jewish scholars begin to go back to their own heritage and history. Some like Geoffrey Hartman and Harold Bloom began in traditional literary studies and turned more to their Jewish heritage. In some ways, *our*—for am I not speaking of myself?—collective cultural silence in the Anglophiliac world has poignantly (and maybe, we should say, pathetically) mirrored that of some Holocaust survivors who tried to bury the past. I am thinking of survivors who seem to have successfully put behind them the concentration-camp universe, only to find out that the experience cannot be repressed or sublimated. Now some of us want to use the skills we have learned to reconnect to our European antecedents, whether they were immigrants generations ago or are Holocaust survivors.

Jewish intellectuals realize that the discontinuity in their history created by mass destruction was not only a human loss, but also a generational gap—indeed, an epistemological gap—in their actual and metaphorical lineage. We want to close the gaps in the vertical relations not only with our parents but our children as well. Realizing perhaps that our own survival depended on a geographic accident, we want to understand the plot that might have been. In Anne Frank's pictures we see our children, our nieces and nephews. We try to build bridges in our memory from our world to the Holocaust's inexplicable *erasure* of history as well as from our world to what might have been had European Jewry continued to flourish—and we inevitably fail in both endeavors.

Holocaust studies has not only developed in the wake of ethnic studies, but has become a centerpiece, an essential field. One can almost say it has the cachet that women's studies had a decade ago. Indeed, Jewish women who had obliterated their ethnic identity when becoming active in the women's movement, are now often in the forefront of those re-examining their Jewish roots and the Holocaust. The *Times Literary Supplement* (*TLS*), which barely mentioned Jewish studies for decades, and patronized Jews when not ignoring them, overflows with reviews and discussion. More than Marcel Ophuls's *The Sorrow and the Pity* (1969) and Claude Lanzmann's *Shoah* (1985), Green's teleplay series *Holocaust* (1978) and Spielberg's *Schindler's List* (1993) brought the Holocaust into popular consciousness. Generous donors underwrite Jewish studies the way they once underwrote Yeshivahs in Israel. Book publishers compete for Holocaust studies because they sell. Museums, photography, books, and films feed upon one another and whet the very appetite they are meant to sate. Psychoanalytic critics have focused on the effect of trauma upon the memory of survivors and how it affects the children of survivors.

For some Jewish scholars the Holocaust as subject along with questions of Jewish identity, assimilation, and the moral implications of Zionism may be the bridge to participation in cultural debate and engaging a larger audience. Put another way, Jews as literary intellectuals are discovering a way to be not only public intellectuals but also self-identified and proud Jews.

Note

1 I have neither the space or inclination to add to Susanne Klingenstein's overview of Jews in the Academy in her two fine studies: *Jews in the American Academy: The Dynamics of Intellectual Assimilation 1900–1940* (New Haven, CT: Yale University Press, 1991), and *Enlarging America: The Cultural Work of Jewish Literary Scholars, 1930–1990* (Syracuse, NY: Syracuse University Press, 1998). Perhaps I should say that I don't always agree with her programmatic division of Jews into various academic generations.

5

Professing Literature in the Twenty-First-Century University

I. The Idea of the University and the Economics of a University

Let me begin with the poetry of the university. The university mission is to expand fields of knowledge. In the sciences, particularly in biology and chemistry, expansion of knowledge will lead to longer and better lives. In psychology discoveries may help us understand why we behave as we do, and, in the social sciences, they may lead to a better understanding of how we make decisions. In the humanities, the benefit of research is more intangible but it may improve the quality of our lives to learn more about the forms and contexts of literature, music, and art and, through history, to learn more about humankind's past and who we are. Thus, in their research component, universities also serve the interests of the public.

We need to stress, however, that universities do far more than research. They grow young people. How do they do this? By teaching them to reason, to read critically, to write lucidly and deftly, and to speak articulately so they can participate as citizens in a democracy and develop into community leaders. We need to teach our students the joy of learning, the pleasure of discovery, the gratification of thinking independently even as they share the process of thinking with brilliant minds in action on the page and share that process in the classroom with their peers and teachers. Teaching at its best fosters the excitement of a student knowing his or her own mind is working at its fullest potential.

Universities need be communities in which a major focus is upon dialogue between faculty and students. We need to be idealistic about our potential for creating communities of inquiry where for four years students allow their minds to take a picaresque adventure through courses, libraries, projects, and ideas. We need to remember our clients are primarily our students and our role is to give them the tools to fulfill their intellectual and creative potential.

We also need to consider the function of the university in our democracy. The university—and in particular the great (and not so great) public universities—played a major role and still plays a significant role in class mobility in this country. The GI bill of 1944 provided educational opportunities for returning World War II veterans.

Pressure to compete with the public universities—including the awareness after the Manhattan Project that the physical sciences (notably theoretical physics) required the input of Jews—was a major factor in the elite private universities' opening doors and windows. But in the decades following World War II, other factors included a growing sense (met, to be sure, by resistance) that universities need tap the potential of all Americans. This was fueled by the fact that people of all classes and ethnicities were serving together in the armed forces and the concomitant surging civil rights movement.

The family histories of both my wife—a retired professor—and myself reflect the way that universities opened the doors to ethnics on their faculty. This process began with those whose last name began or ended with vowels (Irish and Italians), continuing through Jews (a subject on which I focus in my chapter, "Eating Kosher Ivy: Jews as Literary Intellectuals"), women, blacks, and other hyphenated Americans. Some colleges and universities—including leading institutions in the University of California and CUNY systems—were also more receptive to the physically disabled, gays, and others with differences notable by dress—Orthodox Jews, observant Muslims, Sikhs—than the elite private universities.

For the most part, despite well-intentioned scholarship programs, private universities have become enclaves for the wealthy as well as for the children and grandchildren of their own graduates. By creating an educational meritocracy that runs closely parallel to class distinctions, such policies run counter to the university's traditional role in breaking down economic barriers. Admissions offices often know which applicant's family has the means to make contributions. The average income of Ivy League parents is astonishingly high, although the statutory colleges at Cornell with their lower tuition draw upon a more diverse group.

The good news is that the wealthiest universities, including the Ivy League ones, do use blind admissions—that is, admissions people do not make decisions on the basis of whether students have means—and try to provide adequate financial help for the less advantaged. And more and more colleges are offering merit scholarships.

Coming from a family whose opportunities derived from the public college system in New York City from which my father was a first-generation college graduate, I favor opening doors and windows to an economic and socially diverse student body. One of the more moving aspects of a recent Cornell graduation week for me was the banquet of a program called the Cornell Tradition. Here families of modest means gathered at a relatively simply barbecue to honor students who had received significant financial aid. The parents were not wearing Armani and Gucci apparel.

II. The Economics of the University

Let us now turn to the economics of the university.

The question is whether the kind of idealistic teaching and research opportunities in the humanities I have been discussing will continue to exist in a world where tuition is rapidly rising and universities look for patent royalties to pay the bills. The answer is mixed. On one hand, elite universities have been the beneficiary of gifts and grants that make such careers as I have had possible. On the other, at many colleges and universities, more and more hiring takes place at lecturer, instructor, and adjunct level, and these ranks do not have the opportunity to build professional careers.

Even if we at times feel that too much of our attention is focused on the business of the university rather than the poetry of the university, we need to acknowledge that financial matters are central to a modern universities and to ask what effect that has on universities. Andrew Delbanco recently remarked in a fall 2007 *New York Times Sunday Magazine* issue devoted to colleges and universities:

> Universities create jobs, develop new therapies and technologies and train America's young people for the modern knowledge economy. All this is true. But comparable claims could be made for a pharmaceutical company. What makes the modern university different from any other corporation? There is more and more reason to think: less and less. (www.nytimes.com/2007/09/30/magazine/30wwln-lede-t.html? ref=magazine)

I think he oversimplifies but is on the right track in seeing the contemporary university as very much a part of the economic system rather than a separate enclave.

Contemporary universities operate within an economic paradox. They need public and private money to supplement tuition, but they do not mirror business in producing profits in terms of services or commodities. At the end of the day, trucks do not back up to buildings to take away the widgets that have been manufactured. Compared to business models, they often lack accountability in job performance among staff and faculty. Yet when they do their jobs, they add to the nation and the world the immeasurable assets of functioning and lively minds.

Universities are far less structured than businesses. Faculty determine who teaches what subjects with the faculty it has at its disposal. In fact, department chairs—or, depending on the department, their designated associate chair, director of undergraduate study, and director of graduate study—make these decisions in consultation with faculty members. Faculty operate in enclaves, and in some sense each enclave has between a small handful of members with common interests and as few as one member. Faculty pursue their own research, usually make the rules for their courses, absent themselves for professional obligations and accolades as well as consulting, and basically within their courses do what they feel like. In exchange, faculty cede most other decision-making of any consequence to the college and university administration.

Put another way, the faculty and the administration have a modus vivendi, in which in return for no supervision of how and where faculty members spend their time, the faculty let the administration do what it pleases, especially in the budgetary sphere. To find where power resides, to quote from what Deep Throat allegedly said during Watergate, "Follow the Money."

We know universities are businesses, even the non-profit ones, and we know economic issues drive their management and administration. Just like other non-profits, they cannot operate without sufficient funds. Many academic decisions are disguised economic ones. At some universities, even student-loan programs and study-abroad programs are administered with an eye to profits. According to Diana Jean Schemo

> At many campuses, study abroad programs are run by multiple companies and nonprofit institutes that offer colleges generous perks to sign up students: free and subsidized travel overseas for officials, back-office services to defray operating expenses, stipends to market the programs to students, unpaid membership on advisory councils and boards, and even cash bonuses and commissions on student-paid fees. This money generally goes directly to colleges, not always to the students who take the trips. (Schemo, 2007)

Today's universities live more with an eye on the bottom line than in the past. Thus the basic requirement of such ventures as Cornell (and I would guess other) Summer Adult University—whether with courses held on campus or in exotic places—is that they cover all their operating costs, including administrative salaries and program operating costs. While, according to the administration, 75 percent of the clients are Cornell University alumni, most of the other 25 percent—all but three or four percent—have some prior connection to Cornell as friends, relatives, or local residents.

Like Cornell, many major universities also run a continuous series of exotic educational trips all over the world; targeted to wealthy alumni, their purpose is to tighten the ties with alumni. The primary business activity of universities is raising money, whether from private donors or state legislators. Especially at private universities, well-compensated development directors and alumni affairs directors develop an enclave and a culture distinct from the intellectual life of the university.

Which departments flourish depends in part on their capacity to bring in outside research grants, in part on their ability to attract majors, in part on their standing within a given institution (which in turn may be based on how the department is regarded nationally). Some fields are cheaper to build and maintain than others. For example, English departments require little lab equipment, teach many service courses, and have on balance lower salaries than other departments, in large part because professors—unlike colleagues in business, law, economic, and information services—do not have non-academic alternatives competing for their services.

Using available data from a range of public universities, Ronald Ehrenberg has recently shown that differences among salaries at these universities have become much more pronounced in the past 20 years. Thus the average full professor salary in Business exceeded that in English by 15 percent in 1985–1986 and by 46.5 percent in 2005–2006, and assistant professors in Business now make more than twice what their counterparts in English make. According to the 2005–2006 figures, only Philosophy, Fine Arts, and Foreign Languages trail English in salaries, and Social Scientists and Math full professors make on average 118 percent of English salaries. Perhaps thinking that lack of secrecy provides some constraints on huge differentials, Ehrenberg hypothesizes, "Publics probably have smaller salary differentials by fields than do privates" (correspondence with me, June 25, 2007).

At one time Cornell published salaries by rank and college, but now has moved to a system of obfuscation because salary differentials by fields and colleges—including differentials within the College of Arts and Sciences where the English department resides—have become so large. According to Ehrenberg, who served as Vice-President for Academic Programs, Planning and Budgeting at Cornell, "The university does belong to data exchanges where they get average salary data by department and they use this with the deans in figuring out how large salary pools should be by department. But this is very confidential information and faculty never see it" (correspondence with me, June 25, 2007).

In the following paragraphs, I shall use available information about Cornell salaries as examples. In the light of Ehrenberg's research we can assume that in most cases Cornell figures are paradigmatic of salary issues at leading universities. The mean figures for Cornell, collected by the American Association of University Professors (AAUP) and published in the March/April issue of *Academe* are misleading because they are broken down only by endowed colleges, that is those supported in large part by endowment—including Business, Law, Engineering, Architecture, Art and Planning, Engineering, Hotel, and Arts and Sciences—and Statutory colleges (those supported in large part by New York State statutes) rather than a college-by-college breakdown which would be far more accurate. Yet, despite this legerdemain, they do allow one to see where one stands.

Cornell Deans will point out that Business and Law skews the 2006–2007 mean for Cornell Endowed colleges of US$141,900 for full professors, US$99,100 for associate professors, and US$85,900 for assistant professors, but the small number of Business and Law professors in relationship to the total number of professors in the College of Arts and Sciences would not pull up the average that much. After 40 years, I have never reached the mean for the endowed colleges—in 2005–2006 I missed it by seven percent—even though I am led to believe I have one of the higher salaries in my department.

As economics has become more foregrounded in university life, power has become more centralized. In my 40 years at Cornell, power has moved upward from department chairs to college Deans to the Provost and President and, for major decisions, the trustees. Deans have more to do with appointing department chairpersons than they once did, and chairs are more accountable to the Deans and they, in turn, tend to do the bidding of the central administration.

In my experience department chairs often have limited managerial experience and are easily manipulated by the Dean and his staff. Chairs who do strongly object to the way Deans do business become ex-chairs. In former times, the Deans of the College of Arts and Sciences at Cornell were far more independent than they are now. When a recent Dean of the Arts and Sciences objected to the university's putting vast resources into a genome project that he felt might jeopardize the interests of some traditional departments—because among other things, it entailed appointing quite a few new faculty members to departments outside Arts and Sciences—he was dismissed.

For those interested in the economics of universities, I recommend *Tuition Rising* by Ehrenberg (2000), although his notion about the power of the faculty contrasts sharply with my experience—that faculty spend a great deal of time meeting as if they had power, but that ultimately they are just beating their wings or, to use another metaphor, think they are making rain when all they are doing is meeting.

The elite universities—several of which are now engaged in billion-dollar fundraising campaigns—are wildly successful at fundraising. For example, Cornell is in the midst of a US$4 billion campaign. Much of university life—from inauguration ceremonies of presidents that resemble the installations of minor potentates and Trustee and Council weekends to graduation and reunion weekends when the grounds are spruced up—is directed with fundraising in mind. Even the annual reunions, with their focus on classes with five-year intervals after graduation, are primarily fundraising projects with the goals of not only building further ties to the university, but of evoking from the alumni of each of those classes a large class gift. The administration and trustees of major private universities are reluctant to share that fundraising success with their faculty. The exception is recruiting and retaining those they perceive as superstars—a phenomenon that has become far more hectic in recent years as prominent senior faculty who received degrees in the 1960s and 1970s retire. In the early 1990s, during the several years of Cornell's last major fundraising campaign at a time when the stock market was booming, the faculty was asked to take minuscule raises.

Most of my humanist colleagues do not have a sophisticated grasp of economic matters. Each faculty member assumes that he is doing better than his peers without having any idea of the department or the college salary scale. Private universities keep salary data as secret as possible; at Cornell, this secrecy has if anything increased. Departments and colleges do not announce mean or medium raises—or senior administrators' salaries, which are outsized by faculty standards. Even Cornell's statutory salaries are not published.

Secrecy dominates every discussion of salary; the Provost wants every Dean to think his college is doing better than its peers, the Deans want department chairpersons to think their departments are being treated well, and the chairpersons assure every department member—particularly those in the upper echelons—that they are doing well.

In my experience faculty across the board within the College of Arts and Sciences are notably inept at looking after their own economic interests and highly unimaginative at contesting what they are told in terms of faculty salaries. During the stock-market decline at the turn of the century, it would not have been unthinkable for Cornell to tap a tiny percentage of its endowment to bridge the gap between stock-market returns and incoming funds so as to underwrite large faculty raises. But, even if a few faculty members were aware of the possibility of drawing upon the endowment, the faculty did not raise this point in an organized or effective way. Interestingly, private foundations but not universities are required to spend at least five percent of their endowments to maintain their tax-free status (Ehrenberg 2000, 269).

Watching for years their salaries drop in relation to their peers at other universities—and being told that one reason was that the cost of living in Ithaca was lower, although much of their discretionary income is spent on products (including airfare and travel expenses) that cost the same or more in centrally isolated Ithaca—the Arts and Sciences faculty finally organized itself and put together an effective committee that went around the then President to the Board of Trustees. The driving force was a long-overdue petition signed by a high percentage of the most distinguished and better-paid faculty. Finally, we had a significant salary-improvement program. But, lest readers think it contradicts my view that the faculty is virtually powerless, this exercise of faculty power was unprecedented in my 40 years here and depended on an appeal to the conscience of multimillionaire trustees who did not want to see Cornell's name spread over the media as stingy to its faculty.

Universities are very concerned with how they are perceived by their rivals and often make decisions that speak to college and university ratings in the popular press. Universities engage in follow-the-leader bidding wars while they are slow to acknowledge the accomplishments of its own faculty members who carry out distinguished teaching and research for decades. In their quest for fame (which is not always the same as a quest for excellence) universities are in the grip of a frenzy to hire perceived stars and are willing to pay enormous salaries—or at least what we regard as enormous salaries by academic standards. Except for presidential, Provost, and Deans' salaries and professional school salaries in medicine, law and business, most academics have a frog's perspective on economics—that is, looking up to what constitutes significant money—in relation to the business world.

In my own English department, as I suspect elsewhere, egalitarian salary models prevailed through the 1970s and well into the 1980s in part because of the leftist political bent of its members. Indeed, in the English department in several universities I know a bit about, far too little salary distinction has been made among those first-tier scholars who do not go on the offer merry-go-round—what I call the "R. and R. cycle," that is recruitment and retention—as if the newly recruited and retained faculty were necessarily better than those who whose performance has excelled for decades but who don't go fishing in the R. and R. lake. At least some of those recruited stars in the humanities are actually limited in range and benefit from a blind follow-the-leader syndrome that makes a field or a figure within a field "hot."

At present star faculty—and some who are designated stars because they are leading lights in emerging fields where standards are not fully established—are recruited at off-scale salaries. In these cases, universities make special arrangements—usually negotiated in secrecy so only the Dean and his associate deans, the department chair (and perhaps a few confidants) know—for reduced course-loads and, at times, for reduced committee assignments and administrative responsibility as well as more research assistance and perhaps secretarial support than their colleagues. Some universities require little teaching at the undergraduate level from their recruited stars.

Because career advancement and prestige depend on finding a supportive enclave whose letters of recommendation will earn one grants as well as recommend publication and tenure, younger faculty tend to form stronger attachments to professional groups and weaker ones to their home institution. Fewer professors plan on staying at the same place for their entire careers, and that is the result of the R. and R. cycle. The wisdom among faculty a generation younger than I is that one needs move to get one's just deserts. With younger faculty more interested in their professional enclaves within and outside the university and less loyal to their institutions, and with power flowing ever more strongly to the central administration where budgetary decisions are made, one can see that the faculty governance role within universities will continue to decrease.

The result of a system that makes business decisions in retentions and recruits outsiders with outsized salaries and perks is a diminishment of loyalty. What does it mean now to be a faculty member of a literary department at a major research university? Within the academic world that I see and know, teaching and working with students struggles for attention with career aspirations. Much of this stems from the mostly accurate perception that only publications play a role in tenure decisions and salary rewards. In the last decades career ambition has increasingly taken precedence over teaching. Many of my colleagues feel greater loyalty to professional organizations outside the university than they do to the university itself. Some people are so intent on writing themselves out of the place employing them that they husband their time to the detriment of commitments to students, especially undergraduate students since graduate teaching carries far more prestige and is a way to put one's name out there in the profession. In my own department, the members of our very strong creative-writing program refuse to supervise creative honors theses, in part because they are convinced they are overworked.

Universities may be hotbeds of liberal politics—as some of the public imagines—but in fact universities are very conservative and take relatively few initiatives in the way they are organized and managed. In my experience Deans and chairs, with the exception of pursuing the laudable goals of faculty diversity, are more likely to rearrange than to innovate, and many operate on limited knowledge of all the facts. At the behest of faculty members they defend the status quo, fine-tune details, and avoid controversial decisions. Faculty members want to operate in their teaching and research as independent units—albeit in the social sciences and physical and biological sciences, they often work collaboratively—and do not appreciate any kind of intervention. Other than basic financial support, faculty members have little administrative expectations or needs and are accustomed to and rather prefer benign entropy. While we can measure to some degree faculty research output and teaching efficacy, I believe that—unless a department or college devolves into complete chaos—it is difficult to measure administrative effectiveness. Businesses can cite profit and loss, but what can Deans cite other than that they preside over departments that are teaching well and doing effective research because the Deans are not intervening too much?

How do departments—to say nothing of universities—undergo self-examination to see if they are fulfilling their mission? Every so often—I think it is stipulated every 10 years at Cornell—departments undergo outside reviews, usually preceded by elaborate self-study. In my experience, the outside reviewers come from similar departments and share the same assumptions about teaching and research. Indeed, our department had a say in choosing the list of possible evaluators.

The evaluating committee may look down from a steep and icy peak and see fissures in the mindscape, but they don't really ask essential questions, such as whether the academic personnel are being used effectively to give the students the best possible learning experience, whether political correctness is dominating hiring and teaching, whether a spirit of intellectual curiosity and freedom exists, and whether faculty members are given the time to do research or whether their days are consumed with endless rounds of meetings. While a great deal of self-study goes into this process producing an enormous amount of paper, this is an instance—quite common—in my experience of the signifier being the signified: in the 2003–2004 academic year we went through this process and an outside committee did a report and its epistemological and semiological meaning is that we went through a process and an outside committee did a report.

With a plethora of college and university committees, faculty live under the illusion they are more powerful than they are. Many spend a great deal of time on these committees and/or on the faculty senate, but decisions on salaries, budgets, faculty lines in departments—whether a department is permitted to grow or consigned to shrink, whether outside appointments will be encouraged and at what rank and salary—and tenure are primarily made at the college and university level.

For example, most of the appointments available to my Department of English over a 10-year period in the 1990s were in what are called emerging or burgeoning fields—American Indian studies, Asian-American studies, black studies, gay studies, postcolonial studies with a focus on Anglophone literatures in former British colonies and dominions—and were part of a laudable process of increasing minority faculty. Our experience was no different from other leading departments and other departments teaching western literatures, although the focus in French departments was of course on Francophone literatures.

In many cases, if we wanted to replace retiring or departing faculty, we needed to hire the minorities for whom lines were allotted. Nor were lines allotted for minority positions in traditional fields but rather they were restricted to emerging fields in which identity politics played a strong role. Thus often curriculum decisions made by our department in terms of course offerings to our undergraduate and graduate students were shaped in part by ideological decisions made beyond the department, although we enthusiastically participated—often with colleagues in other departments since some of the aforementioned positions were joint appointments—in the final choices within administratively set parameters. All this would have been great had we also been able to sustain our traditional curriculum, but because we couldn't replace retiring or departing professors in traditional fields, our curriculum suffered. For example, the fields of romanticism and early American literature, once leading lights in our department, have somewhat lapsed.

Let us further explore the canard of faculty power. The Deans can overrule faculty committees on most issues if they so choose. Similarly, the central administration—the Provost and her several Vice-Provosts—can overrule the college. Basically the faculty has no significant role in choosing a President and a Provost. When a recent Cornell President was, after a brief term, fired by the trustees, the faculty was neither consulted nor did they receive a full explanation of what happened. While confidentiality was cited as the reason, much more could have been revealed if the faculty had been treated as adults.

Departments do admit their own graduate students, but undergraduate admissions does not report to departments but to the College Deans. Many faculty members may sit a few hours a week on the college committee making decisions, but their input—and the decisions made in their presence—are often overruled for any number of reasons, including affirmative action, the putative needs of athletic coaches, alumni connections, and the desire to please faculty as well as staff by admitting their children and, on occasion, grandchildren.

Universities depend greatly on their non-academic staff for support and some of the senior administrative staff salaries are higher than faculty ones. Nevertheless, more often than is current practice, university presidents need stress to their non-academic staff that they are assets when and only when they make the things happen to make the university a better place of higher education. For some years some senior members of the technology support group at Cornell operated under the assumption that their role was not merely support but the equivalent or more important than faculty teaching and research functions. While the fundraising staff raises far more than their salaries and thus can be said to alleviate the continuing push for higher tuition, the enormous increase in overall staff throughout the university—far greater in my 40 years than the increase in faculty and students—adds dramatically to the cost of tuition. In my experience, on occasion, employees in housing, fundraising, parking, or even campus police, lose sight of the fact that the university is about faculty and students, and that meeting faculty is one of the reasons alumni return. In my own department, the department administrative manager has for decades conducted on occasion her own reign of terror at the expense of those faculty members whom she does not like—when she is not merely condescending to them. Thinking that she is indispensable to them, in part because they believe only she can manage a staff or a budget, the chairpersons turn a blind eye to her not treating all faculty with respect.

III. The Function of the Humanities Professor in the Contemporary University

In a May 21, 2004 *New York Times* editorial piece entitled "Why We Built the Ivory Tower", Stanley Fish argued that we should simply do our research and teach students how to follow in our footsteps. Morality, Fish argues, at a university should be limited to teaching students not to plagiarize. If we teach them our subjects, we do our job. If his point is that we should not try to convert them to our political ideologies, I concur. And while it is admirable that students work in the community as tutors to the disadvantaged and that colleagues teach pro bono at prisons, I do not think we ought to make public service a prerequisite for degrees or expect faculty to spend time doing eleemosynary work or performing public service. Later on many students will find other ways to give back to their communities by serving on library, museum, school, university, and hospital boards—or serving as city and town council persons—and doing volunteer work.

Concerned about the introduction of political correctness in the classroom, Fish has been arguing that a college professor's job description is limited.

> 1) to introduce students to materials they didn't know a whole lot about, and 2) to equip them with the skills that will enable them, first, to analyze and evaluate those materials and, second, to perform independent research, should they choose to do so, after the semester is over. That's it. That's the job. (Fish, "Tips to Professors," 2006)

Specifically he is taking issue with Acting and Former Harvard President Derek Bok's 2005 book, *Our Underachieving Colleges:*

A Candid Look at How Much Students Learn and Why They Should Be Learning More, which argues that colleges should: "[H]elp develop such virtues as racial tolerance, honesty and social responsibility"; "prepare [...] students to be active, knowledgeable citizens in a democracy"; and "nurture such behavioral traits as good moral character" (quoted in Fish, "Tips to Professors," 2006).

In our age of PowerPoints, listservs, and computer Blackboards, let us not forget that great teaching derives from a human voice and personality talking passionately and clearly about a subject that she or he knows a great deal about and wants to share with others. While I am sympathetic to not turning the classroom into a staging area for political pontification, I think Fish's view is limited. If he wants to contract the teaching job to a narrow disciplinary perspective, I want to expand it to a more inclusive one. We need to cultivate intellectual curiosity—one of the great gifts teachers can share with our students—and that certainly fits into "the genuine pleasure of intellectual inquiry" about which Fish speaks. But intellectual curiosity goes beyond that; it is the zeal to know about the world in which we live, to want through our reading and our own experience to understand how other people have lived in different times and how they live in different places. And by living, I mean what they live for, what they believe, and what they think. One of the very recent salutary developments in the field of literary studies is that we read about other cultures rather than just about a slice of western culture, and we think about what we read in a more global context. Offering a literature course revolving around recent Nobel prizes would be one way to help students have a window into worlds beyond their own.

We need, as I have mentioned, to teach our students to read critically and imaginatively, understand implicit and explicit arguments, write lucidly and precisely, and speak articulately and coherently. Much of that task falls upon professors of English, but, ideally, it should be shared across all disciplines. As professors of the humanities, we need to expose our students to a wide range of cultural experiences— theater, museums, music and dance performances, poetry, cinema, architecture—by making them aware of what exists in our own academic community as well as in the city or town in which the college or university is located. But we also need to encourage our students to expand their horizons beyond the geographical site at which they study. Of course this mission need not be limited to humanities professors since professors in the social sciences and the sciences may have different perspectives and different books and cultural experiences to share.

Giving our students the opportunity to study abroad—and to do so in a wide range of countries—supplements what we can provide on campus. Allowing others to study in different US sites—say, Washington, DC, our political capital, or New York City, our cultural and financial capital—may be a way of complementing their campus experience. For those who remain on campus for four years, we need to think of their local experience as extending within a radius of 300 miles of campus.

I also think there are ways teachers are role models and it is naive to think otherwise. Students observe and learn from our behavior, just as they learn from others with whom they are in contact, and just as we learn from our friends and colleagues and learned from our mentors. We need not politicize the classroom to demonstrate behavioral paradigms. To be sure we all have quirks and idiosyncrasies, and part of a student's learning in colleges and universities is figuring out what to take from the people he or she encounters.

Students learn by example, and we set that example by the integrity with which we prepare our classes, the fairness with which we grade and uphold standards, the way we use our time, the thoughtfulness with which we teach our students, how we keep our professional commitments (hold posted office hours, read written work conscientiously, and hand back papers promptly), how we passionately and insightfully speak about our subject, as well as the way we take an interest in our students as young adults and the kindness with which we respond to their individual needs. By the latter I do not mean sacrificing grading standards or believing every excuse but, rather, knowing students as individuals and listening to what they tell us about their thoughts and feelings.

In the same piece to which I have referred above, Fish speaks of the need to separate real-life urgency from academic urgency: "To academicize a topic is to detach it from the context of its real-world urgency, where there is a decision to be made, and re-insert it into a context of an academic urgency, where there is an analysis to be performed." But there is a third kind of urgency, perhaps the most important, and that is the growth of the individual student into a mature functioning adult, able to make rational decisions and to enjoy the full benefits of the world in which he lives. This third kind of urgency takes aspects of both real life and academic life into the learning process, or put more precisely, realizes that academic urgency is a component of real life urgency. Each student lives his or her own *Bildungsroman,* and we as teachers are characters in their narrative, whether we choose to be or not.

Modifying James Carville's advice in 1992 to his fellow Clinton supporters, "It's the economy, stupid," I sometimes think we need signs on our desks that read, "It's the students, stupid." We need to convey the passion of curiosity and the joy of knowing. Recently, we hear and read that students learn more from the university experiences outside the classroom than they do within. Even if this is true—and I am not sure it is if we understand the classroom to be what a student puts into his courses in terms of reading, writing, and thinking—we should strive to challenge our students within our courses not only to learn material, but also to present well-organized arguments in written and oral form—and to do so lucidly and precisely—and to read with tact and discrimination. We need to give them opportunities for independent study projects that enable them to see how far they can take their curiosity, knowledge, passion, and interest. We need find a balance between survey courses that introduce students to a smorgasbord of a field and more highly focused courses that enable them to explore subjects in depth.

We need think about a consumer-oriented curriculum rather than a supply-side curriculum; in the latter model we offer only what our teachers wish to teach—often obscure material from their own research—rather than what the students want to learn. But we need to balance this with some respect for what as academic professionals we feel that they should learn. Syllabi that reflect the narrow research interests of the faculty member are paradigmatic examples of disregarding the interests of our student-clients in favor of the teacher's preferences. When we place such specialized courses within the undergraduate curriculum, enrollment is often slight because our clients vote with their feet by choosing other courses.

All of us need to continually keep in mind the answer to a hypothetical student question, "Where is this course going?" Those vetting the syllabi of inexperienced teachers—whether graduate assistants or newly hired assistant professors—need be sure the teachers have answers.

Increasingly, within humanities departments, major universities allow graduate students to invent their own freshman courses. We need to be sure our graduate students organize their courses effectively and explain to freshmen the rationale of their courses. Often in such courses I see no shape to the pudding, by which I mean an underlying premise that a freshmen could follow or that the teacher could articulate. Our freshmen cannot make sense of the mélange— like the popular song *Mambo No. 5*, a little bit of this and a little bit of that—of primary readings, films, critical theory, and, on occasion, music that sometimes comprises the syllabus. Such syllabi are one reason that by the next term most students, in my experience, cannot remember the teacher or the course in freshman humanities.

Every graduate student teaching her or his own course is not my pedagogical preference. In these freshman courses we should have a common curriculum—at least 50 percent in almost every course—so that staff and students have something in common. I have seen data that this makes for better teaching and learning because teachers and freshmen reading similar material discuss it with one another.

IV. Changes in the Profession of Teaching Literature

The way we were

When I entered the profession, English departments at even the elite universities included only a handful of scholars on whom a department's outside reputation depended. The rest did the bulk of internal work—worked, so to speak, in the department's engine room—were conscientious and sometimes quite distinguished teachers, and pursued their scholarship on the side. The second group was promoted to full professor and the first group was given endowed chairs. This division of labor was quite unlike science departments where virtually everyone pursued research programs and successfully competed for external grants, often from NSF (the National Science Foundation). What has changed is that, with lower teaching loads and more leaves, all literature professors are expected to have significant research careers.

When I entered the profession, most colleagues had similar graduate educations, with a strong base of canonical English and American literature and a more specialized knowledge of one part of that literature which was the base of their teaching and research. Now we no longer read the same texts or live by the same conceptual assumptions about what close reading is. This affects graduate education, where it is possible for a student to get a PhD without showing that she or he can teach a text to freshmen in such a way that they learn essential reading skills. Given that teaching is what most literature PhDs aspire to, we need be sure that our graduate students have the necessary skills to teach reading and writing as well as lucid thinking and conceptual synthesizing.

The concept of significant form was once a given; form signifies meaning and perspicacious readers can uncover the intricacies of form to arrive at an understanding of a text. Put another way, texts reveal their nuances and secrets to those who know how to find them. Formalism itself has been called into question in recent decades, often replaced by criticism with a political agenda—whether it be Marxist, Foucauldian, postcolonial, feminist, anti-racist, or anti-classist—that seeks to find in texts issues that show its relevance to that agenda.

In the face of the challenge to formalism, many important questions are being often overlooked. Can we still say, as I have been saying for decades, that the significant form of texts teaches us how to read them? To what extent does the valorization of the concept of significant form by those who claim to eschew political ideology mean that they buy into a particular view of art in which the commodity is aesthetic form?

131

Does an author have the ethical and moral responsibility of using significant form in the service of progressive values? What if he espouses racism or fascism or sexism or homophobia? Can we ask an artist who has mastered significant form to be responsible and accountable for what significant form does in terms of effects on readers? Can excesses of style—overdeterminism—or a dearth of meaning—underdeterminism—be part of significant form? Can meaning be differential in the sense that some parts of a text mean more than others? If we are aware of correspondences to an author's life, especially if the text's aesthetic—as in the "Scylla and Charybdis" passage of *Ulysses*—calls attention to reading texts as an expression of the author's life, does such biographical data violate a formal approach or does it (as I would argue from my pluralistic perspective) supplement it?

The way we are

We are in an era of transition when the very nature of literary studies is being redefined. In a period when we have radically different ideas about what constitutes literary scholarship, some colleagues believe that criticism advances teleologically and whatever is most recent is better. Some members of that group dismiss colleagues and students who disagree with them as ideologically resistant.

We have a great deal of disagreement about what constitutes excellence at every level, whether it be undergraduate or graduate teaching or appointments and tenure decisions. While this has a generational aspect, it also has a field aspect. Those with a bent towards cultural studies seem far less impressed by close reading than by ideological and historical arguments and are, at times, more impressed with statistical evidence of the kind that used to be restricted to the social sciences.

Within some enclaves, reading the same theoretical texts and accepting the same assumptions homogenizes the personal voice and creates a kind of critical monism—be it deconstruction, New Historicism, postcolonialism, or whatever—where proponents and their students begin to sound alike.

What do we mean by teaching?

Teaching is more than coming to the classroom, giving a lecture, and grading papers. Teachers are the building blocks of each student's future intellectual edifice.

Teaching is an art that involves personal skills, the ability to listen and care about the people one teaches, the ability to empathize with what it is like for young students who are trying to balance a vast array of demands on their time. By their command of the texts they teach, curiosity, passionate love of subject, and commitment to students, teachers inspire and enable.

We need to recognize that teaching is an art that develops over time. We would not want a second-year surgeon to operate on us, but we often put inexperienced teachers in situations for which they are not prepared, such as lecturing to a large class. Most departments do precious little mentoring of teaching after faculty members are hired. The assumption is that that our hiring grants teaching prowess the way the king once magically cured scrofula by the laying on of hands.

In my experience, most assistant professors are extremely generous with their time and more responsive to students than experienced faculty members, perhaps because they still identify with their students. In some cases, they are evading their writing by immersing themselves in an endless cycle of conferences and committees, some of which are busy work. Other junior faculty members are at times stingy with their time, perhaps because they cannot afford to be generous, given the pressure to publish. Assistant professors should be assigned teaching mentors from among a department's best teachers. Those mentors can help young faculty members find a balance among teaching, advising, and research and help them maximize preparation and grading time as well as give them suggestions for using classroom time effectively and developing teaching styles.

I was once told that the difference between high school and college or university teachers is that the former teach students, the latter subject. I would argue that this is a false dichotomy and that what we need to do is have a sense of audience—individual and collective—when we teach our subject to college and university students. We need remember that we are growing young adults not growing young academics or any other particular species. This means—particularly during the recent decades when the job market for university professors of English has taken a significant downturn for all but minorities—that we don't measure our success in terms of how many of our students are interested in graduate school, a measurement that some of my colleagues still make.

As one of their courses during both terms of their senior year, our Cornell English senior honors students do an independent study project on a subject they choose in consultation with a mentor culminating in an essay of 50 or 60 pages. We should not, in my view, conceive such an independent project or indeed the English major as necessary preparation for a graduate program and a professional career—although it may be that—but as a process that builds intellectual confidence and self-sufficiency that will be a valuable tool in whatever endeavor the student pursues. Many of our best honors students go on to success in other fields, be it medicine, law, finance, or business as well as secondary teaching and administration. We should also be aware that our honors students know the perils of the job market for PhDs, and make other career choices because of this. To be sure, some may return to academics after a few years of pursuing other paths, but we should celebrate success in other fields as much as we do the success of our students in academics.

Truly, universities develop not only the next generation of academics but also the next generation of leaders. If our students learn to think independently and to work effectively with others, as well as to read, write, and speak effectively, we have taught them a good deal. Of course, finally much depends on their own motivation, but this is something teachers can encourage.

Grade inflation

Let us turn to the issue of grade inflation within the university system and, in particular, in those regarded as the leading universities. At Berkeley in 1963, my wife made Phi Beta Kappa, an honor reserved for the top 10 percent, with a 3.25 GPA. At Cornell in the early 1970s it was about 3.5, now it is roughly 3.9. What I used to give as a B+, maybe a strong B, has become an A−, and I am regarded as a stringent grader. B+ used to be an honors grade. I see courses where virtually every student is given an A and the default grade is A−.

I raise the issue of grade inflation because there is an intangible relationship between slack teaching and high grades; if we give high grades students are more accepting of unprepared classes, superficial reading of their papers and exams, undue absences, and the like, and are not as aggressive in pointing out teachers' shortcomings on evaluations.

We know that all courses that grade high are not taught by slack professors and that upper class seminars have higher grades than introductory lecture courses. We also know that studies clearly indicate that those courses which give high grades—and in many colleges and universities the students can now find mean grades online—are magnets for enrollment.

Grade inflation has its winners and losers. The losers are often the students who would get high grades under a system that made significant grade distinctions. With the collapse of grading distinctions, standard tests take on greater importance, and the pressure on students to do well on these texts increases exponentially. Law schools fall back on LSATs, Medical schools on MCATs, graduate programs focus on GREs, and employers pay less attention to grades.

Dealing with troubled students

Let us consider briefly an aspect of teaching that is not in our job description, namely responding to students in need of psychological help. Often, because of class size, humanities faculty members are in the front line in locating troubled students. For many freshmen, their only class under 50 students is their writing seminar. Part of growing young adults—which I define as our job—is to recognize when a student is in pain, whether from substance abuse or anorexia or debilitating depression. Students are often crying out for help and do not know how to ask.

135

On rare occasions I have had to deal with severely aberrant behavior. Usually such behavior takes a self-destructive mode. Faculty members need to be alert to students who are suffering depression and have some guidelines about what to do; they need be aware of such signs as slovenliness, fatigue, moodiness, and poor posture. Rather than try to be amateur psychologists, we need to refer students to the campus mental-health professionals and follow up with calls to the appropriate Deans and clinics. In rare circumstances, I will call parents if no one else will, even if technically I am not supposed to.

Every campus has suffered the trauma of suicide and such events—like accidental death—ripple through an academic community. Students need counseling because in many cases it is their first brush with death. I have never had a student commit suicide, but I believe in interventional behavior in the form of, if necessary, walking a student to the health center's psychiatric center or driving to the psychiatric ward of the hospital.

Students who are 18 or older are considered adults and cannot be confined unless they are arrested because they are a danger to others or agree to be institutionalized. Their civil rights sometimes are at odds with the community's needs, and they do not have to accept parental intervention.

Quite a few years ago I received a letter from a student whose grasp on reality was very slim but who, in the midst of a rambling psychotic document, threatened violence to herself and two of my colleagues. I immediately contacted the psychiatric services and the advising Deans and steps were taken to track the student until her parents arrived to take her home. After receiving instructions on how to use my desk as a shield if I were attacked, I met with her. But people trained to use physical restraints were outside my office. More recently, a splendid student in our department—one who came to every class prepared in the two classes she took from me—stopped doing her work and disappeared. The appropriate university authorities got a court order to enter her apartment to be sure she was alive. It turned out she was having a relationship with an older man off campus.

After the Spring 2007 massacre at Virginia Tech, do we need more administrative guidelines on how we handle peculiar and aberrant behavior? The Virginia Tech catastrophe is one all universities fear. I have had a few very peculiar students, and in my 40 years two or three who desperately needed help. Vigilance is important in understanding the difference between the eccentric and the truly dangerous, and sometimes proactive measures are necessary to separate someone who might harm others from the community. But sometimes it is hard to know just what to do. If Kafka had handed in "The Penal Colony" or even *The Trial*, would we not have thought he was psychotic?

Evaluating teaching

We need to try to understand what makes a classroom work and we need mentor our younger teachers even while ensuring that our senior teachers do not become complacent or stodgy. I would propose to have established senior faculty members who have been honored for their teaching visit the classrooms of younger teachers once a term during the assistant professorship and once a year before promotion from associate to full professor. Some departments do this but such visits are contrary to what we have always done in my department.

How do we evaluate teaching? One question that should be asked by a department's faculty (and not only in tenure meetings) is "Would I want my children to be that teacher's undergraduate students?" Can we trust undergraduate students to know if they had a good experience? Perhaps we should complement anonymous surveys on the final day of classes, when anxiety about grades and finishing assignments runs high, with anonymous exit surveys before graduation.

For the evaluation in the fourth year that takes place before formal tenure review and again during that review, we solicit letters from students whom a candidate has taught. Students enjoy writing on behalf of teachers who have been important to them and whom they admire. When they don't write, they are voting with their hands. A response from undergraduates of over 20 percent is considered excellent and a positive sign of enthusiasm.

Although departments tend to give them greater credence, graduate students' letters are often less reliable and less disinterested than those of undergraduates because the students have a vested interest in teachers and mentors being promoted. Colleagues and grad students have been known to nudge other grad students to write encomiums. Some graduate letters are just cheers for what graduate students are doing and anxiety that the person who is mentoring them will not receive promotions or accolades.

Discrepancy in productivity and performance

Many of my colleagues are terrific teachers, scholars, and intellectuals, but my concerns in this section are directed to performance inequity among colleagues. It is my belief that we hold faculty to far less demanding standards than other professions, particularly in those fields where grant reviews are not part of regular evaluation processes. We need recognize that some people work and other people talk about working.

Our department has never had a faculty manual spelling out responsibilities, although one is now in the works. Letters of appointment here and elsewhere not only need to spell out what is expected but the annual salary letter needs a paragraph reminding faculty members that teaching undergraduates and mentoring students on honors projects as well as independent study is a main reason why they are here. I say this at the same time that I recognize the generosity of many, including most of those I regard as the department's real achievers, who balance distinction as a teacher, citizen, and scholar in admirable ways. These colleagues understand that the academic community culture— an intersection of department, college, and university citizenship— and the culture of real achievement can and should go hand in hand.

Paradoxically, as teaching loads have dropped and research support and salaries have increased, dissatisfaction has increased among faculty members. In part this is the result of breaking into enclaves—or what I call balkanization—where we do share a common pursuit. Enclaves within departments develop in which the interests of the enclave often take precedence over the interests of the department. I am not saying that, in former years within English Departments, the Medieval program or American Literature or Creative Writing didn't have its own sense of identity, but now the balkanization is much more pronounced. In large departments, where colleagues don't have regular contact with one another, except at department meetings—which are not always well attended—colleagues regard those who disagree with them not as intellectuals with valid points of views but as caricatures or parodies.

We need remind those who complain that teaching at a university is a lot more fun and a lot less difficult than digging coal with a pick. Indeed, complaining and whining (as often as not an offspring of the culture of professional achievement, including the anxiety about one's own place in that culture) has reached unprecedented proportions. This results, frankly, in some people not doing what they should be doing; good faculty citizens take up some slack, but at times egregious non-performance affects the quality of the teaching and advising product we offer our clients—that is, our students.

To be sure promotion and salary increments are the rewards for good performance, but the best professors do not foreground this in deciding what to give to their students and university. Clearly many colleagues who reside in what I call the "complaining group" also are (in varying degree) often generous with their time. *But* it is imperative that newer faculty members do not find a place in the community of complaining; those of us who believe in community culture need to help. In fact, while our department has something of a mentoring system, the mentoring is all too often based on reinforcing the very careerism I am criticizing.

Slack teaching performance and shoddy citizenship relate to a culture where perceived public acclaim is the measure of merit. It does not help that the current generation of Deans and department chairpersons grew up in the world where merit is measured in terms of public acclaim—although that acclaim can often be the cheering of a handful of outside people within a small field who depend for their careers on reciprocal cheering.

Indeed, I teach in a ranking department where the disparity in work output—measured by productive teaching, commitment to university activities, and publication—is extraordinary. I also have worked with a few tenured colleagues who are one-tenth as effective as others and little effort is made to either correct, retrain, or make arrangements to retire these people, some of whom have been tenured for decades. A few full professors—who would never have been promoted today from associate professor but were promoted in more lax times— have allowed their writing careers to lapse and even have neglected their teaching responsibilities.

Over my 40 years in the profession, I have seen little willingness on the part of department chairpersons or Deans to deal with problems of alcoholism, depression, and chronic illness. Rather they take the path of sticking their heads in the sand and ignoring these problems which interfere with how faculty do their jobs. I have had a few colleagues who for years could barely do their job. Of course, this leaves some students without competent or even functioning teachers. In my experience, department chairs are untrained for many of their tasks and often rely on non-professorial internal administrators to make decisions about faculty matters.

I have on occasion asked myself why, recused as we are in upper New York State and with ideal working conditions, some of my colleagues are not as productive as some of their peers in terms of their output as either scholars or creative writers? I sometimes fear that in recent years we have too many meetings and group occasions (including subgroups across departments and even fragments of those groups) and too many weekend conferences as well as lectures and readings and all the concomitant social occasions. Are all these afore-mentioned activities good for younger colleagues (and graduate students) if the activities collectively pull them away from the two activities—teaching and writing—which are the essence of what is, and must be, a somewhat lonely and introspective (but satisfying and wonderful) life?

Professorial slackness takes many forms. Failing to grade and return papers at all does occur. Often the prompt and timely reading of student papers takes a back seat to other tasks. There is no excuse for not returning undergraduate papers within a week, particularly at university where a reader or teaching assistant is provided for classes of any size.

Preparation for class at times is shoddy. Some faculty members miss scheduled office hours, cut classes, and do not answer emails from students. Some faculty do not make the effort to learn the names of students even in smallish classes of 15 or so. I have had colleagues who are absent far too much and one who spent so much time traveling and giving lectures at other universities that students spoke of that teacher falling asleep in classes.

The supervision of graduate students is hardly exempt from faculty slackness. Faculty postpone for months the reading of graduate papers, especially late papers—which they often encourage by giving incompletes too readily—and dissertation chapters. Other examples of behavior that is not necessarily in the graduate students' interest is allowing them incompletes that stretch on for years.

As Department Honors Director during four recent years, I was disappointed when faculty declined to mentor honors essays in fields other than their own because it could mean doing a little extra reading that might deflect them from research time. There is far less prestige in giving attention to undergraduates than graduates. Yet undergrads—especially the best ones whom we designate as Dean Scholars in the College of Arts and Sciences or as Presidential Research Scholars—nowadays sometimes choose Cornell with the idea of working with a particular person.

Why should a first-rate honors student work with someone far from her area when we wouldn't ask that of a first-year graduate student who is one year more advanced? Students tend to want to work with professors with whom they have studied—just as graduate students do—and if their topics were framed in a course on the Decadents they usually don't want to work with a Spenser scholar.

I have colleagues who routinely turn down all requests for undergraduate independent study, although most will take on any graduate student for that is where the prestige lies. In my role as Honors Director, I had to pester faculty members assigned to be anonymous graders of honors essays to return their graded essays, even though such delays might affect the students' getting the honors they deserve. Giving a reasonable percentage of our major students the opportunity to do sustained independent work is a way not only to recruit our share of excellent students to Cornell but also to recruit some of Cornell's best students to our department. Of course, this is also true elsewhere.

141

For some colleagues working with honors students does not carry the prestige that working with graduate students does, and this means some give this activity less effort. The need to reward those who give their time to undergraduates has not been fully addressed at major universities where teaching loads give the truly able enough time not only to write but to teach in the fullest sense, including spending some time taking students to plays, museums, and concerts; taking an interest in their extracurricular athletic, musical, and dramatic activities; having meals with them at their dining facilities; and teaching them how to do research in labs as well as archives and rare-book rooms.

When considering the idea of a university, the subject with which I began this chapter, we need think, too, about what the university should be doing to infuse our students' education with intellectual energy and to give undergraduate students a chance to work independently under the guidance of professors who meet with them one on one.

6

Reconfiguring the Profession: The (Uncertain) Path to a Professorship

In this chapter I shall be speaking to the next generation who will be the heirs to the profession that I entered 40 years ago. My subject will be graduate study and career development.

I. Career Embarkation: Applying to Graduate School

Academic cultures, like many other cultures—and especially elitist Mandarin cultures—tend to replicate themselves. When I was an undergraduate, the best students were made to understand that they were acolytes in the academy and were made to understand they were the chosen ones who were fortunate to be considered by their teachers as candidates for graduate school and for careers as college teachers. Gradually—as I discuss in my chapter, "Eating Kosher Ivy"—the concept of "best student" came to be expanded to include those who as scions of working-class first-generation Italians and Irish, and, later, Jews and women, might not have fit the original replication criteria. It was like being tapped for the novitiate within the Catholic Church. You were made to understand that you were one of the Elect.

Now with the academic base including more diversity and with even most Caucasians now committed to diversity, the academic world has become less like a secret society. But given the difficulty in the job market in most literary fields, who should be going to graduate school? There are strong variations within the market; Spanish literature is still a field with job opportunities—in part because of the greater number of Spanish-speaking students, in part because of the increase in Latin American studies—whereas comparative literature is a very tight field. Burgeoning or emerging fields—such as queer studies, ethnicity, English or French literature in former colonial countries—are good areas to pursue. Minorities are very much in demand, especially in the aforementioned fields since many universities and departments have made diversity a high priority.

Let us consider as professors how we should mentor our students to apply to doctorate programs. I would make the following suggestions to doctoral applicants in literary studies:

1)   Learn about the programs to which you are applying and when you write your applications, show some familiarity with the program and the faculty.

2)   Apply widely—15 schools are not too many—because admission is very competitive and the best candidates apply to many of the same top schools. The best schools have hundreds of applications for a handful of places. At Cornell, our English department had 431 applicants in 2007, 461 in 2006, 432 in 2005, and 388 in 2004. With grade inflation, graduate record exams (GREs) take on great importance. In 2007 our department admitted about 35, shooting for an entering class of 14. In 2007, for our Creative Writing MFA (Masters in Fine Arts) program we had 352 applicants—about 100 for poetry-writing and the rest for fiction-writing—and we admitted 10 for eight places; in 2006 we admitted nine of 324 for eight places.

3)   Be aware that when choosing among candidates for admission, graduate programs are aware of the job market and know that minority students working in burgeoning fields are more likely to get jobs.

4)   Know that students who take a year off after graduation and thus wait a year often are more successful in their applications because they have graduated with distinction and can cite graduating with honors as a qualification. They can also list on their application Phi Beta Kappa and any senior prizes they might have won. Graduate

schools will be impressed by a summa cum laude or a magna cum laude honors degree, particularly from a fine undergraduate program because such a degree is a good predictor of graduate school success. Waiting a year means that faculty recommendation letters will include specific comments about honors essays and other senior work.

5)   If you are not admitted to one of the top 10 programs, it is quite possible that you can transfer (or reapply) with a masters. Furthermore not every college hires from one of the top 10 programs; small colleges often prefer people with degrees from strong regional universities in the same geographic area as the college. Thus students who want to teach at college but do not want to be major scholars may do just as well with a degree from a solid program that is not in the top 10 or so, although one should note that more and more small colleges are requiring publications for promotion—a trend which may be good for the paper industry but not necessarily for the quality of higher education.

6)   If you will only be happy teaching at a major school on the East or West Coasts, I would advise you to think about doing something other than pursuing a doctorate in literature. Many fine jobs are in the hinterlands and restricting oneself to the coasts limits the possibilities of finding employment.

II. What Happens in Graduate School

Let us turn to graduate education. Grad school is many things, but among them it is an academic labyrinth—a series of exercises—through which students pass on the way to their professional Bar Mitzvah or Communion. We need to regard graduate study not as a career phase but as a transitional period from undergraduate to professional, in which two of the most important lessons are how to find worthwhile research projects and how to use time effectively.

In their first few years, students take courses and select those faculty members who will constitute their doctoral committee. While the form of the committee and the time in graduate study when the committee is constituted varies from university to university, the chair of that committee will supervise the student's dissertation.

At Cornell we have not only permitted the oral qualifying exam to be limited to a small number of works proposed as much by the student as the faculty but we have also substituted a variety of procedures for comprehensive field exams. In the past the purpose of the exams was less to examine graduate students at the end of their third year than to give them a list of essential works to read in the fields in which they plan to teach and do research. Although these field exams generated some anxiety, I regarded them as quite effective. Students have always been so fearful of anything that is called an exam that they will accept any proposal that seems to compromise it. Because students do not want to write field exams on a reading list, we now allow them to write time-consuming essays on topics they propose, and these essays are much more burdensome than simple exams written for a few hours a day for three days. And then we wonder why they are writing dissertations in their seventh year or beyond.

But is the abandonment of oral qualifying exams as a diagnostic exercise covering an overview of English and American literature and of written traditional field exams—supplemented by an oral component—in the students' interest? It is not the exams but the preparation that matters and, as has been the case in the past, I would expect close to a 100 percent passing rate since that was the case when we had such exams. For many students, the most valuable part of graduate education other than the dissertation itself was the field exams; the second most valuable was the qualifying exams. From the former came the ability to teach survey courses and from the latter came grounding in the field in which one teaches upper class and graduate courses and in which one writes.

In fact, it is not in the students' interest at all to take qualifying exams on a few works of their own choosing and substitute more elaborate and time-consuming procedures for field exams. I would return to separating field exams from the dissertation and have each committee member give an exam taking about four hours, and I would have these exams taken within the period of a week. Over the years doctoral study has become a career in itself, in part because of the discouraging job market and in part because rather than give students a working map to get through the labyrinth, we have on occasion ceded our teaching authority and entered into elaborate negotiations with the students about what they should be doing. Now, in an era where students have input in the shaping of the processes by which they are evaluated, our department allows graduate students to fulfill their comprehensive field exam requirement by writing a dissertation proposal or by writing long essays in answer to their own questions or constructing a syllabus or developing an annotated bibliography.

III. Choosing a Dissertation Topic

Let us turn to choosing a dissertation topic since that choice defines the field in which you will be looking for a position and the area in which you will most likely make your first important mark as a publishing scholar. Look for problems and issues that need investigation. Think boldly. You need to show theoretical sophistication and awareness of recent criticism. Write well and that means write lucidly and succinctly, avoiding dissertationese and gibberish. You should not write jargon— whether it be Cornell-speak or Yale-speak or Foucault-speak or Cultural Studies-speak—that is impenetrable to anyone but your committee and a handful of graduate students working with some of the same people.

Choosing a topic that makes a contribution to a community of inquiry and at the same time sustains your interest is an important skill. Remember there is a difference between a dissertation and a thesis; a dissertation needs a thesis, that is, a sustained argument based on marshalling evidence.

In the Spring of 2007 I asked a number of colleagues at major universities what kind of dissertation work was being done there and how it related to success on the job market. Even when the dissertation foci were thematics and representation that in some cases seemed to drift into the non-literary, I was struck by how burgeoning or emerging fields and postcolonialism carried the day.

In some departments or pockets within departments, narratology is still at high tide or it plays an important role. I am thinking of the Aristotelian projects of James Phelan and his journal *Narrative*. Narratology can be used to supplement other approaches as in my *Imagining the Holocaust* where it plays a pivotal role in my discussion of the distinction between what happened and how we remember what happened, and the distinction between what we remember and how our telling gives shape and form to that memory. Once we understand that temporality within the visual arts is different from the diachronic shape of narrative, narratology can be used more than it has been to date in thinking about the visual arts.

In formulating dissertation topics, keep in mind certain guideposts. Too often today critics can become Neo-Platonists scanning for passages that fulfill their *a priori* theory and neglect the evolving text. In such circumstances, close reading of texts gets lost in a welter of information. Alternatively we have good close reading, but really nothing new in terms of perspective or context so that the discussion is no more than old wine in new bottles. Put another way, following my mantra "Always the text; Always historicize," I suggest trying to bring formalist concepts to the study of burgeoning fields that tend to stress representation and representational investigation to fields that stress formalism.

Burgeoning fields are still excellent areas in which to write whether they be ethnic studies—Asian-American, African-American, Native American—or gender studies or gay, lesbian, and transgender studies, although there may come a saturation point in some of these subfields just as there have in the past been saturation points in traditional fields. Rediscovering figures in burgeoning fields—like Asian-American literature—may work, but I would urge you to write on figures that stand up to rereading and teaching.

Be aware that a Caucasian writing in the field of black or Asian studies is, all things being equal, less likely to get a job than candidates belonging to those minorities and therefore whose own life experiences fulfill the ethnic expectations of the job search. Extraordinarily qualified Caucasians working in ethnic studies have had a very difficult time getting positions.

What especially does the trick is choosing topics that can be placed in the context of large patterns and issues in the field and if possible in the canon beyond the field. In other words, try to move beyond niche writing in these projects. For example, since James Baldwin knew the

African-American, gay, American and even English and European canon, you might show these various cultural matrixes if you were to write about him. Similarly Amiri Baraka—who changed his name in 1967 from LeRoy Jones—was influenced in the 1950s and 1960s by the world of New York City experimental theater and leftist politics.

Within my own field, modernist studies, I think there is much more to be done with the relationship between art and literature as well as between art and music. Word–image projects—comics, advertising blurbs, posters, and graphic novels; comparisons of authors and painters creating at similar times; theoretical projects discussing space and time in different art forms—are still on the frontier, as we have begun to understand that reading now extends far beyond how we respond to small black marks on a white printed page. A number of people, including me in *Reconfiguring Modernism: Explorations in the Relationship between Modern Art and Modern Literature*, have proposed maps for such work on word–image projects; within that area there are still fine dissertations to be written.

In more contemporary or postmodern studies, artists such as Ed Ruscha, Richard Prince, Robert Longo, and Cindy Sherman need to be examined in connection with contemporary literature. Some of the projects intersect with ethnic studies; while Art Spiegelman's marvelous graphic novel *Maus* has been examined as Holocaust literature, has his work been fully contextualized in terms of its contribution to the graphic and comic genres? Dan Morris is doing fine work on Jewish photographers. There is work to be done with the relationship between, on one hand, modern music and modern dance—especially the role of the Diaghilev ballet—and, on the other, modern literature and modern art. Matisse and Picasso only worked together once, as designers in Paris for Diaghilev. (I have written a bit about modern dance in my *Reconfiguring Modernism*.) Taking advantage of the greater opportunity for interdisciplinary training at major universities prepares students for such projects as well as those that wed history and literature. I might add that one need not sacrifice close reading or engage in abstract polemics when pursuing interdisciplinary work of the kind I am suggesting.

149

Another rich area for dissertations is inquiry into the history of a paradigmatic theoretical model—say Foucault or Jameson or Emmanuel Levinas—and how that model has been applied to authors, texts, and issues. How is post-structuralism as a term used differently in the visual arts, especially architecture, compared to its use in literary studies? How is the term "deconstruction" used in popular media? How has popular culture been affected by high culture and vice versa? Do television shows like *Sex and the City* and *The Sopranos* affect high culture and, if so, how? Erasing distinctions between high and low art and focusing on the economic and social production of art, the field of Cultural Studies has become mainstreamed as a centerpiece of literary studies. Cultural Studies has left Marxist literary studies in its wake—or, some might say, returned Marxist studies to its roots as a subdivision of a Hegelian view of history.

Writing on themes and using several writers as examples is in vogue—for example, the lower middle class women in a select group of novels; ecological issues in novels about Africa, including such figures as Gordimer, Coetzee, Conrad, Achebe; and the Potato Famine in Joyce and other Irish writers. I might warn that some dissertations spend too much time with context and not enough with primary texts. They are not so much interdisciplinary as what Marjorie Perloff calls *otherdisciplinary* (Perloff 2007, 655) because the literary is secondary and the paradigms are often taken from other fields such as history or anthropology rather than from formal study of texts or what used to be called poetics. If colleges and universities looking to hire assistant professors are seeking close readers, they may be wary of too much historical background. But there is no rigid formula. I have been involved in a dissertation-in-progress about literature and films about the Vietnam War, and while it is not the first such dissertation, it reaches back into an important historical period and brings that period to bear on the readings it presents in a new way.

In keeping with the current focus on globalization, one possible project would be to look at some or all of the recent Nobel Laureates (say the last decade)—José Saramago, Dario Fo, Günter Grass, Gao Xingjian, J.M. Coetzee, Elfriede Jelinek, Orhan Pamuk, Harold Pinter, V.S. Naipaul, and Imre Kertész—and some of a less recent

150

vintage—Saul Bellow, Toni Morrison, Gabriel García Márquez, Kenzaburo Oe, Derek Walcott, Naguib Mahfouz, Nadine Gordimer, Wole Soyinka, Joseph Brodsky, and Seamus Heaney, and examine what (if any) are the common threads in their works, and what if anything has changed in the artistry and themes of those selected. Is there a particular mixture of the political and aesthetic? Is there a kind of representation that they have in common? Are they chosen because they represent different geographical areas?

I still think—and I am something of a minority on this—that there may be place for single-author dissertations, especially on major canonical ones including Shakespeare, Milton, Joyce, Stevens and Conrad, and perhaps Nobel Laureates such as Bellow. But if you write on Joyce, be aware that Wakeans will probably not be hired by small colleges or colleges without major research programs unless your dissertation shows *Finnegans Wake*'s continuity with prior Joyce. If you trace the career of a living author, the career may change because of major new texts or even expressions of his or her viewpoint in speeches and articles.

English studies have expanded infinitely and a student can write on subjects that in my day would have been passports to obscurity. But you do want to have a dissertation that is appealing to those who hire. Quite a few English departments have students writing on film, but I ask myself would our department hire someone whose stress was on film? Perhaps not, but Theater Arts would. If you do interdisciplinary work in film studies and literature, or art and literature, or Holocaust narratives—one of my fields—you may make yourself more appealing to some departments and less so to others, and that is fine as long as there are jobs in the field in which you choose to write.

I would keep the following in mind when choosing dissertation topics:

1)   Choose a topic to which you are passionately committed. You will be living with this topic for some years, not only while writing for your degree but as the likely source of your first publications and your first book. You need to love your subject and find it exhilarating.

151

2)   Choose a topic which will be helpful in the job market, but this is less important than choosing a subject that engages you. You need a topic that is a magnet, drawing you to your workspaces where you read and write.

3)   Choose a topic with the advice of your committee, and be sure they are fully committed to it and understand what you will be doing. In choosing a dissertation committee, you need to have people who are committed to the project and committed to you not only while you are a doctoral student but also through your career. Don't be afraid to reconstitute your committee or add someone after whatever Admission to Candidacy exams your department requires. Be sure to discuss with your committee frequency of meetings, expectations of turnaround time when you submit material, and what their policy of accessibility is when they are on leave.

4)   Be aware that your dissertation is usually your first book, and keep that in mind while writing it. Remember some readers will only consult one chapter of your study to learn more about a book that they are teaching. Make sure each chapter of a dissertation on several texts or authors is not only a distinct part of the overall argument but that it stands on its own and expresses a miniature of that argument.

Although you need to consider the dissertation a book in progress, be aware that you can finish the book after you finish the dissertation. Small topics yield small or minor manuscripts, and minor manuscripts are harder to publish at a time when even university presses have few expectations of enough readers to break even financially.

5)   Define in your prospectus a project that you can finish in 12 months and be sure your committee understands that there is a timetable. It may take a little longer to finish than a year, but conceiving a dissertation as a year-long project makes sense. Working on a dissertation for too long can not only be psychologically debilitating by draining your self-confidence, but a warning sign for hiring departments of writing block and dithering.

6)   Consider the relationship of your topic to your teaching. Most successful humanists do a great deal of their writing from their teaching, particularly early in their career. But a problem with some

subjects—including more abstract theoretical projects—is their disconnect with teaching. One problem with writing on recent authors—other than those who have been or are in the process of being canonized—is that you may not have a chance to teach them a great deal. To be sure, in this era where departments often let their faculty—and even graduate students—teach anything except the local phone directory this may be less of a problem.

Still, highly abstract and theoretical subjects—say the influence of R.D. Laing on literary studies or the place of museums in late nineteenth-century culture—are less likely to be the focus of the kind of bread-and-butter teaching you might do in your freshman writing classes and in your first full-time teaching positions. While we are not alone at Cornell in being latitudinarian about letting our grad students bring aspects of their research into the freshman classroom, many colleges and university have core courses and certainly do not share that openness.

7)   Keep in mind that, if you go to a college where teaching is stressed to the extent of burdensome teaching loads, you may do some of the best work of your life in grad school because you will have the most time to do that work.

IV. Writing Dissertations

Let me make a few suggestions for the process of writing dissertations:

1)   Maintain a dialogue between reading and writing rather than wait to write until you have done all your research. When you have an idea write it down; if you have just read a work, read some scholarship and try writing an early draft based on your reading. If you have in your research developed an overview of a major critical or scholarly text that pertains to your project, try to imagine where it will fit into your argument.

2)   Keep a computer file that is a letter or memo to yourself about the direction and argument of your dissertation. I keep in mind Auden's line, "'O where are you going?' said reader to rider" with the pun on

rider implying writer. In my experience, one of the most difficult things for young scholars is to go beyond individual analyses and develop a conceptual overview and deft comparisons. The other is to relate historical contexts to individual works in a way that makes the contexts convincingly essential. Stress in your opening pages your argument, method, and contribution and keep referring to these throughout, most especially the argument which you need to tie together as you proceed. Have a nice but short conclusion pulling your argument together.

3) Work every day seven days a week, but do not work all day; returning to your work after a break is like looking at your check book after not looking at it for several days. You forget what was there. During every day, you need rest and respite, fun and frolic, walking and other activities. My sense is that most productive scholars—those who work over a lifetime as productive scholars—work in the morning; those who stay up all night for the most part get less done and look less well as they age.

4) Consult your committee frequently. Do not duck into the restroom when you see a committee member walking down the hall. If you feel a need to avoid your committee, you have the wrong committee for you.

5) At times, it makes sense and is often helpful to leave the main path of your project and read a little bit in a related area. Such reading may become an integral part of the project either by providing context or other kinds of theoretical or historical understanding. But sometimes we make the mistake of going elsewhere in our intellectual endeavors when we cannot figure out how to solve difficult problems. In other words when you get lost in the forest, it is better to recall the main path or locate your compass than choose to pursue putative byways out of the wilderness.

6) While going to and organizing conferences gives you a taste of professionalism and a chance to meet colleagues with common interests, too much of this can become a major distraction. Yes, conferences may be fun, but they distract one from larger projects. The cycle of preparing and giving a paper, and then resuming one's university life on return, takes a few weeks, and often disrupts a project demanding sustained writing. Conferencing is good for networking, but it is not

the same as publishing. For assistant professors, the advice given to me in 1968 still has some relevance: "Stay home and write your book."

7) Don't leave graduate school without a finished dissertation. Put another way, the only good dissertation is a finished one.

V. Interviewing: Some Advice to Job Candidates

A basic rule: The more competitive the job market, the more important the interview process. Preparing for interviews requires a good deal of effort and some understanding of what interviewers are looking for.

Most jobs fall in three categories: 1) major research universities; 2) regional research universities; 3) small colleges or branches of regional universities, both of which stress undergraduate teaching. In all cases read the school catalogue and—especially in category 2 and even more so in category 3—know as much as possible about the place and the city. If you come from an elite university, perhaps preceded by an elite undergraduate college, your interviewers may be doubtful that you will be comfortable in a small town in Nebraska or Alabama.

Successful interviewing depends on self-presentation. Handing out a syllabus or even a page summary of your dissertation, if you think that will be a helpful way to speak about your dissertation, can be a good idea. Some years ago one of my students did the latter on his own, and from feedback I learned it helped him get a good job. Keep a notebook—or computer file—of questions you anticipate and write answers of various lengths (none too long). Include both generic potential questions and answers and ones specific to the hiring college or university interviewing you, and read what you prepared before the interview or before public appearances on the campus visit. Take advantage of any practice interviews with experienced faculty that many departments now offer their students as preparation for the job market. Tape your responses to various questions so you can hear how you sound and then polish your answers.

You should prepare oral descriptions of various lengths of your dissertation; depending upon whether you are interviewing at a small college or a research university, you will be asked different kinds of

155

questions. Be sure you can state succinctly the argument of your dissertation as well as speak precisely about your approach, method, and contribution.

While unspoken as a criterion, most people want a colleague from whom they might learn and from whom their students will learn but also—since faculty are people—a colleague whom they might like and be respected by and who observes the amenities. They know that we all have quirks and idiosyncrasies, but they would rather discover them gradually; put another way, if interviewers see too many quirks at first, they imagine that there are a great many more and that the interviewee might be a little weird.

For jobs at major universities, you need to convince your listeners— and hosts if you are invited for a campus visit—not only that you fit their job description but also that you will bring something that they don't have to the department. You need to read their catalogue and know how you will add to their graduate program.

A good small liberal arts school has different criteria and looks for different candidates than Berkeley or Cornell. Research universities will probably ask you about your next project after your dissertation. Colleges will more likely ask you about potential syllabi. Your teaching prowess and teaching experience will mean a great deal everywhere, but especially to small colleges. Dedication to the college community in the form of participation in the department and college life will mean more at smaller colleges. Such colleges will get nervous about folk who are commuting or have a great desire to be in San Francisco or Manhattan on weekends. Hiring committees can't legally ask about your personal life but be sure to give the impression you'll be there and digging in.

For small colleges that have English departments with a faculty of perhaps 15 members or even fewer, you need to define your areas of expertise broadly. If a small college department chair asks if you can teach Milton for a year while Bloggs goes on leave, the best answer is, "Yes, although it hasn't been my graduate focus and I'll need to prepare." The chair doesn't expect you to be running a grad seminar on Milton or whomever. The college department probably doesn't have a major published scholar teaching Milton or, for that matter, Joyce or

Woolf. You aren't expected to be a world-class scholar on all subjects any more than any one of your graduate mentors is.

For all interviews, prepare in your mind what you will add to the curriculum and what courses you'll offer—including what texts—that are not in the catalogue. You need to remember that the goal in job-hunting is to be the first choice once; having several interviews and finishing as second choice won't do it, unless the first choice, for whatever reasons, turns down the job.

While some departments make offers at the Modern Language Association, the usual goal of an MLA interview is to be invited for a campus visit. Remember, too, that hiring committees at MLA get tired and, even if some of the interviewers are flagging, you need to be sure you present yourself as fully as possible as the ideal candidate for the position. So be proactive and don't get deflected by those interviewing you who start recalling their days at Stanford or Cornell or being in grad school with those who provided letters of recommendation for your file. Remember at MLA you have a half-hour to present yourself, and if someone starts telling anecdotes, they are stealing your time to make an impression. My only suggestion is to smile and, showing a tad of your sense of humor, try to get back to your self-presentation.

You can't know all about a department's political history, so don't try. Be yourself. Sometimes a former student in your graduate school department, who is on the interviewing faculty, will be a friend or advocate. Finally, when you go to the department party of the inter-viewing place—or visit the campus—don't be captured by one or two people but circulate and move away politely from those sharing department or personal gossip. They are not being professional and are often not in the loop. Being the candidate of a faction in a divided department rarely leads to offers.

VI. Academic Careers

Tenure is a lifetime appointment, and because it is, departments need to be very careful about whom they tenure. When I began my career in the late 1960s, major departments hired more assistant professors than they could possibly tenure. Less care was taken in the hiring process because it was assumed that many assistant professors would not be tenured.

Now we hire fewer assistant professors but we have a strong expectation that those we do hire will make tenure. This is in part due to our hiring at a later stage in careers than hiring at completion or almost completion of a PhD; many of our candidates are eight years or more past their BA and some have had various kind of post-doctoral fellowships before being hired. Others have been assistant professors elsewhere for a few years. Thus their careers are more advanced than hires in my first 15 years here, 1968–1983, when we didn't give tenure to quite a few assistant professors. Still, within the humanities, it is sometimes not only difficult to predict future development when hiring as assistant professors 30-year-olds recently out of graduate school, but it is also difficult to see future careers when we vote on tenure and promotion to associate professor.

Before the balkanization of the profession, when colleagues could and would read the candidate's material in fields beyond their own, major articles in prominent journals along with a manuscript endorsed and validated by senior outside scholars was enough for tenure. And the medievalists were at times and indeed still are on occasion exempted from the book manuscript requirement. Now while most departments expect a published book for tenure or at least an accepted manuscript as well as progress towards a second book, some departments want a second book.

Universities and colleges have their own procedures for granting tenure and there is often some variation within departments at each institution. My department appoints three readers to report to the faculty on the research and teaching with the expectation—often more respected in the breach than the performance—that all tenured colleagues will also read the candidate's scholarly or creative material. Two of the three report on the writing, one on the teaching. A number of letters are also solicited from major figures within the candidate's field. For quite some years, the candidate has had input into whom is asked. (Some fields are so small that those who are asked have an interest in a positive decision.) After a provisional vote, the department chair writes a letter to the candidate to which he or she responds before the final vote. The chair then writes a letter of transmittal to the Dean carrying the department's recommendation, which has been in recent years almost always positive.

As I have noted, universities wish to be in the forefront of the academic universe, and that is all to the good. Junior people in so-called burgeoning fields are highly sought after and given special grants and summer salaries that other hires do not get. Yet despite elaborate procedures, not only hiring mistakes but also tenure mistakes are made in such fields, in part because the standards are very much in flux and in part because there is a dearth of qualified candidates. In burgeoning fields, candidates are often tenured without the credentials—usually a published book or one accepted for publication with outside readers' reports available during the tenure proceedings—that would normally be expected. Our department actually hired an editor for a junior person in one of the burgeoning fields because the assistant professor's writing was substandard. Surely, one would expect an English professor to be able to edit his own manuscript, perhaps with collegial input.

One thing that hasn't changed in my time is universities' love of secrecy in their own promotion and salary procedures; probably only Masons and Rosicrucians love secrecy more than academics. Secrecy of course engenders speculation and gossip since tenure decisions are often made on the basis of individual preference by department members voting in secret without having to explain their votes. After this the Dean—knowing to some extent on whom he can count for the result he favors—appoints a confidential ad hoc committee to review the tenure file and report back to him. After receiving the ad hoc report, he may consult his Dean's advisory committee. If a candidate is turned down, there is a university appeals procedure in which elected faculty members provide recommendations to the Provost who has the final say.

On occasion, a department wants to avoid strife and depends upon the Dean's ad hoc committee to make a decision. For example, some years ago I chaired an ad hoc committee where the department vote was, if memory serves, nine yeses and nine abstentions. Such a vote is one way in which a department refuses to come to a verdict.

We need to use the tenure process and later full-professor promotion to examine teaching credentials and to think about who should be teaching such diverse courses as lecture courses, honors seminars, and graduate seminars, as well as who should be nominated for teaching prizes. We also need to recognize that some people can do some things well but not others. Colleagues who can't make small talk or ask "Are you enjoying your freshman year?" and can't answer the kind of questions entering freshmen ask of their freshman writing teachers, shouldn't be teaching freshman writing seminars. Those who cannot give an informative, interesting, and well-organized lecture to juniors taking a survey course in the American novel or romanticism or whatever should be given some other assignment. At times we put barely capable teachers in situations that are not right for them. If someone has become a teaching albatross—leaving confused and tearful students in his wake—and there is no hope of improvement by interventional retraining, universities should offer financial incentives to get that person to resign.

The expectation is that promotion to tenure as an associate professor will—after six to 10 years—be followed by promotion to full professor. The procedures described for promotion are the same as those for tenure, although it is expected that the associate professor's professional reputation will have grown. It should also be expected that the candidate for promotion to full professor has both improved his or her teaching and is playing an important role in the department's graduate and undergraduate programs, but unfortunately those criteria are often not given much attention. When we can't promote an associate professor after 10 years, we are on the way to having a lifetime associate professor, and that means a wrong decision was probably made at tenure time.

In past generations, some universities promoted everyone to full professor after some years, on occasion on a charity basis, and used salary disparities to make merit distinctions. In my department but not in all departments at Cornell, promotion to full professor after some years used to be automatic, but now the college insists on substantial research progress past tenure.

Many years ago when I was on the Dean's advisory committee on appointments, I was a member of a subcommittee to provide standards for promotion to full professor because there was a disparity within the college. Most notable (in part because historians would be on our ad hoc committees and vice versa) was the difference between history's rigor—two books as an absolute—and what some thought of as the English department's less rigorous policy. The idea was as a matter of equity to have similar standards within the college and considerable progress has been made towards that goal.

But having more rigorous standards creates its own problems here and elsewhere. We, like many departments across the country, now have several colleagues who have held the associate professor rank for many years. While some of these long-term associate professors are exceptional teachers, there is a strong tendency for them to become unhappy people who do not add much to the community. Clearly, a mentoring system needs be put in place that helps associate professors move towards full professorship; perhaps in most cases the mentoring relationship at this level may play a relatively perfunctory role, but I know of many situations where it would have been most useful.

While there is still quite a bit of variety in the standards for promotion from associate professor to full professor, the expectation now is that the candidate needs two published books for promotion to full professor or at least a second accepted manuscript in addition to the published book that earned him tenure. Some major places would like some progress toward a third book. While this may make sense at major research universities, does it make sense at colleges where the primary activity is teaching undergraduate students and where there is little research support in terms of either necessary time for research or appropriate funding? Indeed, more than second- and third-tier colleges and universities, the best schools are often more likely to make exceptions to publishing requirements if—and this is a big if— the candidate is involved in a major project. In some cases for promotion to full professor, a major second book is underway or, in the case of medievalists, a number of articles seem to be accepted as a substitute for a book.

When asked to review dossiers for promotion at other colleges and universities, I am asked how the candidate would fare at Cornell. While I often use hyperbole to describe a solid candidate—because hyperbole is the necessary mode to support a candidate—in my private thoughts I wonder if it is reasonable for a college or a branch of a major university to require books when few members of the prior generation have such credentials.

A touchy subject in academics is post-full-professor review. After promotion to full professor, post-tenure review takes the form of annual reports on the part of the tenured faculty to the chair who, within our department, consults a salary committee whose members are not known to others in the department. And the chair provides an annual report to the Dean. While endowed chairs are often used in recruiting and retention, distinguished faculty members can be given these plums as a reward, but in many departments there are not enough to go around. And what, within a major research university where employment includes research expectations, should be done about those full professors whose performance ranks in the fourth quartile—or the tenth decile? Are they called to account or given ample mentoring? Alas, not.

A former Ivy League President refused to even consider formal and rigorous post-tenure review procedures on the grounds that, as I was told, he would lose the necessary faculty support for other initiatives. But my experience tells me that most of the faculty at a top place would like such a plan; indeed it is in place within the University of California system where there are several levels of full professors. Weak full professors muddle along and sometimes are given suitable mid-level administrative jobs within the college or department or university especially if they have suitable personalities and service capabilities. Even an informal system that alerted those whose performance as teachers and/or researchers was sub par would be helpful.

Of course an intelligent and flexible post-tenure review policy would encourage productive and creative professors to move outside their fields to embark on interdisciplinary projects and would understand the difference between small projects and large ambitious ones that might take more time but yield major results.

VII. Succeeding Professionally: Balancing Teaching and Writing

I know I am fortunate to enjoy writing and, indeed, I have branched out (publishing about 65 poems, some travel articles, and a short story), but I know for many people writing is most difficult. I should add that for me, writing can be very hard work and takes great patience and alone-time, and that alone-time makes me more of an extrovert than I would otherwise be when I do come up for air. And the confidence I now have (some days) took a long time to earn and depends in part on the ability (and luck) to choose topics that excite me and interest readers and in part on my efficient use of time. And I have been fortunate in being able to link my teaching to my writing. The irony is that I don't feel particularly productive, but I just keep working and teaching and reading and thinking, and things seem to come together (but far from always). Working on more than one project helps, because if one day I am stuck, I go to something else.

While some academic fields work more collaboratively than others, success as a university professor in the humanities requires a great many hours each day of working alone. For most academics, time is not money; rather, time is time. Department chairpersons and Deans can help, but we need be as efficient as possible in being sure that we have the time to do what our profession is about: 1) teaching—including preparing for our teaching; reading student papers and vetting their projects; mentoring Honor students, independent study undergraduates and graduate students; and writing letters of recommendation; and 2) research and writing.

For many people, working in isolation many hours a day is difficult, and these people find other ways to spend their time—committee meetings, conferences, colloquiums, lectures, and the accompanying social activities. These activities seem to have proliferated tenfold over my 40 years at Cornell and draw some people like moths to a flame. As management expert Peter Drucker reputedly said, we can either meet or work.

Having colleagues read and comment on our writing is important. But is it possible that too much collaborative activity in the form of reading groups and colloquiums dilutes the personal voice and creates a kind of institutional voice and even a disciplinary voice to the point where students and colleagues begin to sound homogenized?

Let us think about an issue that is crucial to a successful academic career, namely continuing to find research issues that are worth pursuing. Many people do not know how to find topics, particularly after getting tenure with their first book, often a version of their dissertation. Some are easily distracted, while others don't know how to focus. Projects can come from any place: carry a notebook everywhere so you can write down your ideas. Assume that anything not written down, or put in a file on your computer, will be forgotten. For the same reason keep a pad on the table by your bed. Even sound sleepers have inspiring moments during the night. In the humanities your teaching can give birth to wonderful writing ideas and there is no reason to separate the two. That does not mean proposing obscure courses that feed directly into your research, but rather writing on the major texts you teach and understanding how the process of reading for your students and your process of rereading might differ.

You may discover that some conferences are not worth your time and effort and that audiences are often tiny; the whole concept of academic conferencing is modeled on the sciences and derives from pre-Internet days when scientists had to exchange information to move work forward. The humanistic homology was always somewhat bogus since we don't need to know what everyone else in the field is doing as if we were studying the whooping-cough virus or black holes. But the homology worked for creating conference funding, sometimes to quite splendid places.

We now have geometrically more conferences in proportion to less need (due to the Internet), and most people would be better off spending their time reading and writing. Excluding the networking function in a weak job market and the social function for people to get together, one main purpose of conferences is self-perpetuation. When I was beginning my career, grad students rarely presented papers at conferences; the profession had very few conferences, and on occasion a scholar passionately, eloquently, and lucidly spoke about a subject about which he or she had thought a great deal—note the parallel to good teaching—as opposed to the current dominant practice of reading a paper (often close to the speed of light) that few can follow. But this was before the proliferation of talks at each major school and the frenzy to create smaller and smaller identity groups for each writer, interest group, etc., and the accompanying frenzy due to the shrinking job market to give papers before finishing grad school. Panels have become larger, sessions shorter, question periods nil, audiences smaller—all to accommodate more and more participants.

An academic career is a marathon not a sprint. In our field, time is not money, but time, by which I mean it is the currency that defines you and how you use it will determine your success. How does one learn to maximize time without becoming compulsive? Recently I was asked to put in writing some suggestions for time management. Without seeming to pontificate, let me repeat here some simple (and hardly earthshakingly brilliant or original) time-management tips, keeping in mind that each person will modify them to suit his own needs and temperament and phase of life. For example, I now have fewer family responsibilities than when I was parenting younger children; my now having a retired wife makes meeting various hosting and housekeeping commitments easier than when I was trying to juggle two careers with my first wife, a public-school administrator.

Some of what follows I learned from watching the legendary professor—and my colleague—M.H. ("Mike") Abrams as well as from observing and talking to many others. These suggestions obviously do not apply to professional traveling or vacation time. Not surprisingly, some echo my ideas for working on a dissertation. While these suggestions are idiosyncratic, they are fungible and can be adapted to your needs:

1) Work every day—seven days a week—but not all day. I might add that many productive scholars take a full day off on one of the weekend days, although I don't, preferring to spread recreation to segments of virtually every day. Spend some part of each day away from research projects and teaching. Have regular routines and keep accurate track of how you use your day. For some, lists and schedules work well. I live by EMC, that is, Every Minute Counts.

165

Avoid all-nighters or late-nighters, which take their toll on how you feel and even look. Do not compensate for days when you do less than you wish by staying up all night the next day.

2)   Awaken early—say 6.30—go right to your workspace, work an hour before breakfast.

3)   Leave your email until you do some real work on your research project.

4)   In the evening, read texts related to your project; this for me stimulates thinking while sleeping. But the last thing you read should be something relaxing.

5)   When not otherwise occupied, work after dinner and quit at 10pm or so.

6)   Prepare talks and papers in advance so you do not mortgage tomorrow by going into sleep-debt today. If you do your work in advance, you'll be ready if you have a family emergency or if some other project—or lecture invitation—comes along that interests you.

7)   Working diligently until lunch followed by leisurely reading and then a nap is restorative for the rest of the day. Personally, after lunch I enjoy reading the *New York Times* (admittedly now the subject of one of my book-length projects), but you could just as well read a book you are enjoying, or that you will be teaching, or that is related to your project.

8)   Except on teaching days, I suggest that grading and course preparation take place after lunch and dinner. In an effort to balance teaching responsibilities and research, I put in extra long days the day and night before my teaching days.

9)   Exercise regularly; for me this takes place after my afternoon work session (which may be teaching preparation and/or administrative/committee work). How one takes care of oneself—even in terms of alcohol, food, regular and necessary sleep—matters.

10)   When traveling, keep up with email and as much academic and personal business as possible, so when you return, whole days are not lost while catching up.

11)   Keep lists; during breaks in the morning and after lunch and rest, I take care of personal business and small job-related tasks (calls, pending emails, recommendations, etc.).

166

12) Enjoy your office hours and interactions with students. They can be splendid teaching occasions. Meetings with colleagues—especially sharing graduate student exams—can be fruitful learning occasions. Beware of colleagues who extend exams and committee meetings interminably, and try to agree on a time limit for all meetings.

13) Spend very little time in idle chatter on campus. I try to be courteous and wish everyone "Good morning," but I limit small talk, even though I can be loquacious when relaxing. Avoid group coffee breaks. Except for business lunches with a specific purpose, I do not lunch with colleagues.

A codicil: When I was younger, I did occasionally have bag lunches with some colleagues, and this social practice does help build community. I have visited departments where colleagues bring bag lunches and get together in a room each day, but on the whole I think one needs to monitor lunchtime breaks. Because I have found social lunches at the Faculty Club that last well over an hour interrupt my focus, I limit those occasions to necessity.

14) Weekends—when email and personal business are the lightest—are great times for thinking and working.

15) Think of home mealtimes as break-times and enjoy them.

16) When you go to lectures and colloquiums be aware of the time investment and ask yourself whether that is the best use of your time.

17) If you live, as I do, very close to campus, some one-on-one meetings can take place at home, and that can be more efficient than coming and going to campus.

18) Enjoy vacations and, unless you have a work emergency, leave your work at home. When I was younger I did at times take proof and copy; editing on vacation, I worked all day. But later I learned that publishing deadlines are often negotiable and when publishers ask the unreasonable in terms of giving you time for these tasks, you need to tell them your schedule and your needs.

19) Insulate yourself as much as possible from the ebbs and flows of department politics. We all worry about the politics of our workplace and our interactions with those deciding on our promotions and salaries, but as much as possible try not to worry too much about these

matters. Some people thrive on tension, others become debilitated by it, but most of us are in between these poles. I myself prefer a very calm sea and, despite the critical wars over past decades, I have—with the exception noted below—found no worse than choppy seas rather than hurricanes and typhoons.

You will have colleagues who waste time exchanging endless memos and gossiping about small departmental matters. You will probably have within a long academic career at least one chairperson that is not as nice to you as you would like or are accustomed to and may even be quite mean spirited to you and others. Some people, as was the case with one particular chair in my experience, savored enmity and seemed to use fissures between herself and her colleagues as driving forces to motivate herself.

You may not even understand why a particular chair is difficult for you to work with. As much as possible, forget about that chair, know his or her term is going to expire, and focus on your work. Realize too that all your colleagues and chairs are not going to be equally appreciative of you and, that if you express strong opinions, some will take umbrage.

Your place in the department may also rise and fall in response to changes in the critical winds, which of course also can become a factor in department politics. Because of my adhering to traditional ideas about humanism, I have at times been written off as obsolete by various colleagues.

20)   Some people draw energy from working on research projects and course development with other colleagues. In literary study collaboration is less common than in some fields, and I tend to work more effectively alone. But every scholar needs a reader whose judgment he or she trusts; mine these days happens to be my wife, Marcia Jacobson, a retired professor of English.

VIII. Retirement

When I began to teach the retirement age for academics was 65, then it was raised to 70, and since 1994 there is no mandatory retirement age. By continuing to teach past 70, faculty members are in effect blocking the hiring of younger professors and contributing to the tight job market. In some departments, the ethical question of appropriate retirement age seems to be foregrounded more than in others but, even within those departments, there are strong exceptions, depending on the disposition of the individual and the institution's desire to retain some stars well past the age that it would like less distinguished people to retire.

Let us look backward to the bad old days when we had a stipulated retirement age. It used to be in my department that when a professor reached retirement age, he or she was immediately moved to a small shared office with all the rest of the emeritus professors. Before remodeling many years later, that office was next to the men's room where one could hear toilets flushing all day. In a rather ignominious process, book carts arrived at the retiring professor's office July 1 for the move. Most gave away the lion's share of the books or took them home, since the shared office could only accommodate a small percentage.

Particularly at the top universities where faculty members are treated well and have not only a good deal of flexibility with regard to how they use their time but also a continuing interest in their research and teaching, there is now a limited incentive to retire. My wife had a chaired professorship at Auburn—including research leave that left her teaching only two-quarters of the three her colleagues taught—but she also had much less teaching and research support, and much less input into what she taught, than I do at Cornell. Had we not tired of commuting, she would have taught some years beyond her 57th birthday, but she was suffering from a kind of professional fatigue, as do many professors at small colleges and those public and private universities where teaching loads are heavy and support is limited.

For most people, the concept of retirement implies an improved quality of life with greater time to do what one really likes to do. But if one enjoys one's life as an active professor what does one have to retire *from* and retire *to*? Faculty at major institutions are more likely to be so immersed in their work that the thought of a different kind of life is a bit frightening. They already have significant time to do

169

what they like to do most, so why give up their salaries and the prestige of their positions to do the same thing that they will continue to do? The more professionally active already travel a great deal, giving lectures and pursuing research at conferences or other venues and the only limit on their professional and personal travel is their teaching 30 weeks or so. In my case, I teach 11 terms out of each 13, with leaves of one sabbatical term and one research term. What are faculty members gaining by retiring at 65 or even 70 unless they suddenly wish to change directions, play golf every day, or move to another geographic area because of the weather or proximity to family?

The assumption of course is that those not retiring are still functioning at a high level. That is not always the case, but the fall-off in teaching and research capacity occurs at widely different times. Some of those who do stay on the longest are those who should retire first, but that is not usually the case. I have colleagues in their 40s who are on the downside, and Professor Abrams, who retired at 70, has, at 95, more energy and ideas than many active professors in their 50s and 60s. In the absence of strong post-tenure review procedures, the question is who—spouse, chairperson, colleagues, or disappointed and frustrated students?—will tell us when we are slipping and thus should be retiring? Most of us tend to think that we are still in our prime while it is our colleagues who are aging.

There is a good deal of economic incentive for universities to want their higher-paid faculty to retire because senior professors can be replaced by less expensive younger ones. Some of the less distinguished colleges and universities replace professors with even less expensive lecturers, some of whom are part-time appointments and very inexpensive.

Yet in many leading universities a great deal of talent and distinction is located in the older faculty and this distinction will not necessarily be replaced by the next generation. In my department most of the luminaries are in their 60s or upper 50s and, while we have a strong group of younger faculty with potential, we may not have the same density of quality in the middle group—despite some excellent mid-career faculty—in part because in those years we did limited hiring except in burgeoning fields, and in some of those fields we stretched our tenure standards because of the dearth of available candidates. I should also mention the concomitant loss of a few excellent people in mid-career.

At Cornell, there has been little incentive created for retirement within the endowed colleges. While each faculty member negotiates his own retirement, and signs a confidentiality agreement, the basic parameters are that those who go half-time by 70 are given full benefits for five years, most notably the TIAA-CREF (Teachers Insurance and Annuity Association, College Retirement Equities Fund) contribution of 10 percent on what would have been their full salary. Of course, anyone who wishes can retire within the five-year period—and thus get even less that the extra 10 percent on half of his or her salary. But, assuming a mean salary for the next five years of US$140,000—with the actual half-time of salary of US$70,000 and extra contribution of 10 percent on the remaining but unpaid US$70,000—the university is contributing US$7,000 a year for a five-year total of US$35,000 extra to retirement. This is hardly significant to senior faculty whose retirement accruals are in seven figures.

At one point in the 1990s after the mandatory retirement age was lifted, one serious proposal focused on capping retirement contributions at 37 years. In fact, the cap for quite a few faculty members would have been 63 or 64 since many of the elderly faculty began quite young. This most incendiary proposal might have led to some of the most distinguished professors finishing careers elsewhere, since the age of academic mobility has significantly lifted, and would also have resulted in some professors changing their wills to eliminate bequests to Cornell because they would have been angry.

One way to encourage retirements, not only in science but also in all disciplines, is to provide offices and workspace for emeritus professors. At many universities, retired science and engineering professors need to vacate their labs to provide space for their successors. Were that changed so that retired faculty could remain professionally active, more faculty in those disciplines might retire.

But at elite universities giving emeritus professors shared office space does not increase retirement incentives greatly. Adding US$2,000 research funds for the next five years after retirement, as Cornell has done, helps a little but far more needs be done to encourage retirements. Former Cornell President Frank Rhodes once said to me in a private conversation—when he was no longer President—that a better policy was at 65 to give faculty five years at half pay and let them do no teaching for those years. Maybe that age should be 70 with the codicil that the faculty member cannot postpone acceptance of this option once he reaches 70.

Conclusion: The Future of Literary Studies

What kind of profession will succeeding generations find?

The future of English literary studies will include continued emphases on globalization and non-western literatures—Asian, African—but also an awareness of how the dialogue between East and West has shaped cultures in both areas. A recent exhibit in the Metropolitan Museum focusing on Venice's dialogue with the Arab world entitled "Venice and the Islamic World, 828–1797" examined "the relationship between Venice and the Islamic world over a thousand-year period, focusing on artistic and cultural ideas that originated in the Near East and were channeled, absorbed, and elaborated in Venice, a city that represented a commercial, political, and diplomatic magnet on the shores of the Mediterranean" (online description).

We have become more aware that arts of some cultures have different purposes than the decorative and aesthetic function of western art. African art masks have practical uses in various tribal rituals; carved pillows and walking sticks signify status. We now know that the borders of art stretch far beyond museums, and we have come to appreciate the artistry of furniture and automobile design, architectural drawings, functional tapestries from diverse cultures—costumes, carpets, and quilts—as well of new digital and video art forms, including popular forms such as clips on YouTube.

The borders that separate the study of national literatures and cultures will continue to break down and our interest in previously neglected cultures and literatures will grow. Such changes will continue to transform the structure of literary departments—which have already undergone considerable changes—with the blurring of distinctions between film study and literary study, theory and philosophy, ethnic literature and ethnic histories, as well as literary and cultural studies in such fields as gay and women's studies. More courses will be offered in literature in translation and the translations will include more exotic languages like Hindi, Urdu, and African languages. Scholars and teachers will continue to worry about the difficulty of applying formal analyses to translations. They will discuss whether the best translation is the exact rendering of the original text or one that captures the spirit of the original or is its own imaginative entity that pays homage to the original's content but is stylistically its own work. But the focus on literature in translation will continue to be on content and—particularly when dealing with more exotic languages—how it expresses cultural and literary history.

We will, I hope, try to reconnect academics with the larger intellectual life of our culture and bridge the wide gulf between the academy and others interested in the life of the mind. For example, we should be seeking new terms to carry on global discourse; but if we wish to play a role in shaping the actual world, we need to be sure we address issues without jargon.

Certainly we shall continue to have canon reformation, but I want to argue for the centrality—if fluidity—of a literary tradition stretching from Chaucer through Shakespeare and Milton to Joyce and Woolf, from Phillis Wheatley through Herman Melville and Nathaniel Hawthorne to William Faulkner and Toni Morrison. And, if pressed, I would side with those who want to focus on reading literary texts rather than those who would focus on teaching the conflicts within modes of interpretation, but I don't see why we cannot do some of the latter even while stressing the former.

I strongly disagree with those who are tolling the death of literature because young readers are uninterested in close reading of poetry and sustained reading of serious prose. I do not see any evidence of this lapse of interest in my students. My hope is that we do not lose sight of the pleasure that reading brings by transporting us to different worlds where we hear the voices of dramatized others not ourselves. We must stress, as I argued in Chapter 1, the beauty of a wonderful passage, the wonder of significant form, the sensuality of words—all of which are evoked by Wallace Stevens' phrase "ghostlier demarcations, keener sounds" ("The Idea of Order at Key West"). Nor should we forget the centrality of the artist who, no matter how impersonal art seems, has created the literary text—or a musical piece or painting—by making choices deriving from inspiration, thought, and deliberation, and giving shape to the meaning and effects of his work.

One of the important tendencies in the past few decades is the proliferation of book clubs, most of which read serious contemporary texts and some of which read canonical texts or a mixture of contemporary and canonical texts. The liveliness of such clubs shows us that books have not been displaced by the Internet and continue to be a source of pleasure, trouble, controversy, and interest to people outside the academic world. In a healthy way, book clubs blur the line between inside and outside the academic world. To be sure discussions of *Ulysses* within clubs devoted to James Joyce might not have the sophistication of a graduate seminar, but does that make so much difference in the pleasure of reading—and the concomitant social and intellectual exchange—to group members?

Shaped by the Internet, our criticism and scholarship will often be more collaborative—even though each of us may be working alone at our computer—along the lines of Wikipedia (the online encyclopedia composed and modified by anonymous contributors) and various listservs where dialogues take place among scholars on specific topics. The Internet is an essential underpinning to information globalization and brings conflicting constituencies to the same site. Yet it also can inform discussion with a kind of populism which undermines expertise and authority and pretends all opinions are equal. In terms of literature, it may undermine hierarchies and establish new ones in which major canonical authors are considered less important than J.K. Rowling and the Harry Potter books.

What will happen to literary criticism in the age of the Internet? One can only speculate on possible changes. Will each faculty member be expected to maintain a public blog? How will the blogosphere change publication expectations? Will an assistant professor's tenure be in part based on a combination of how many hits that person's blog receives and how often he or she is quoted by other blogs?

When communicating on the Internet, the need to reach beyond one's own culture may have the effect of minimizing jargon, but, on the other, if every subgroup retreats into its own listserv and blogosphere, we could have even more balkanization and specialized jargon.

One apparent downside to the Internet blogosphere and discussion sites is what Andrew Keen has called "The Cult of the Amateur," where gate-keeping is undermined and what we think of as knowledge becomes more and more subjective because the lines between fact and nonsense, between expertise and rant, become blurred. He makes a compelling case that the Internet—at least at times is "undermining truth, souring civic discourse, and belittling expertise, experience and talent" (quoted by Cohen 2007; see Keen 2007). Amazon.com type of commentary may undermine the stature of a professional class of critics and literary scholars.

Let me close by thinking not only of what might happen in the world of literary studies but what I think should happen. We academics need to participate in public discourse and engage not only our peers in other nations and cultures, but also the non-academic public on the issues that concern us. Certainly Henry Lewis Gate has bridged this gap in presenting African-American literature and defining—by his range, depth, perspicacity, and, most importantly, his lucidity—his place as a public intellectual. In the 1980s the insistence on Derridean and Jamesonian discourse did not always ennoble Cornell and other major universities as a place open to the free play of pluralistic discourse, but rather at times created an exclusionary, elitist, and intolerant culture from which fine minds even within the academy were excluded. The role of public intellectual may require a new sincerity, a new authenticity, and a retreat from the stance of deconstructive *picaro* that some have embraced. For example, the noted literary and cultural critic's Stanley Fish's online blog and occasional columns for the *New York Times*—questioning established truths on the right and left—have established him as a serious public intellectual and provocateur.

If we use less jargon—and maybe even show a tad more humility—we have a chance of re-establishing ourselves as public intellectuals and rebuilding our link to others interested in examining culture, including the journalists interested in artistic expressions within our culture. What we have now is an immense gulf between the media, including most journalists, and academics. They each turn the other into a parody; journalists often think academics can't write or synthesize and only burrow deeply as if they were doing mole work. Academics often think that journalists do not have the necessary learning and judgment to make subtle distinctions or provide necessary background.

Obviously academic interest in popular culture—whether it be sports or hip-hop—is a way to bridge the gap between literary intellectuals and the reading public, but only if that interest takes the form of lucid discourse rather than abstract theorizing. We will continue to focus on cultural phenomena beyond literature and to blur the line between high and low culture, and between other cultural texts—food, fashion, bodies, sports, laws, wills—and literary texts. Clearly the rise of the graphic novel and the interest in comic books and cartoons—and other word–image relationships, especially on the Internet—will be a focus in coming years.

I do think discourse that takes us too far from what is happening in the actual world and from terminology in which many (perhaps most) intellectuals are comfortable—to say nothing of those outside the academy who are also more a part of intellectual life than we sometimes realize—is a mistake. Not infrequently I hear and read theoretical perspectives on postcolonialism by those who do not know the first thing about contemporary Africa—its disasters as well as its successes, its democracies and kleptocracies and often a mixture of the aforementioned in the same place—and have never set foot in the countries they are discussing. I would hope that literary scholars will, as some but not enough do now, read current events in more than a superficial way, and theorize and generalize from a command of factual information.

In place of the cultural imperialism of one or another approach, I would hope that we realize that a healthy pluralism—a dialogue among discourses and a willingness to read with diverse approaches—works best for understanding a wide range of literary texts and cultural issues in terms of a global perspective. Perhaps we will understand the subversive, ironic, and parodic as stances and voices among many other possible discursive modes and not as the only ones within a full intellectual life. In the borderland between theory and method, we will be asking how older and newer formalism has merged into the New Humanism.

While we need to have respect for synthesis and theoretical hypotheses, we also need to have less undue speculation about remote causes and more research into the factual underpinnings of what happened in the past along the lines of Adam Hochschild's *King Leopold's Ghost*, his splendid discussion of the conquest of the Congo by the Belgian King Leopold II, who used the Congo as private fiefdom through a non-governmental organization, the Association Internationale Africaine, of which Leopold was the sole shareholder and chairman. Such investigation gives ballast to discussion of Conrad's scathing indictment of imperialism in *Heart of Darkness* as well as to glib accusations that Conrad's text is racist. Put another way, we need less speculative synthesis and more synthesis based on facts. We need be wary of postmodern theory with its emphases on seeing gaps and fissures, and its desire to propose ironic or hybrid explanations that fit only small samples of data and overlook the rest.

We need to situate ourselves politically and geographically—acknowledge who we are and what our project is—before we read texts as if they were history. It is all very well to speak about the end of nationalism, but it is clear that nationalism is still the dominant political discourse (and what our own immigration debate is about as well as what similar debates in Europe are about). How we read texts about contemporary events—say Nadine Gordimer's *The Pickup*—depends in part to which imagined political community we see ourselves belonging. A radical Islamist would find the book offensive, but so might a feminist who would resist Julie's willingness to adjust to a culture in which women do the work and are in a subservient position.

Explanations of turmoil in the Congo or genocide in Darfur—where, to be sure, the oil interests of the West and China are factors—or Africans exploiting Africans, do not necessarily need to be explained solely in terms of western imperialism. Hochschild's text makes us aware of what happened in the Congo but we need other explanations to understand why 50 years of independence have not fulfilled the promise of postcolonialism. For example, Paul Theroux's *Dark Star Safari* (2003) shows us what Africa has become, in part because of corrupt leaders, well-meaning but ineffectual charities, deluded evangelists, tribal warfare, and natural disasters. I suspect that we shall have more awareness that colonialism is not the only cause of current complex problems in Africa and parts of Asia but one cause among many.

Postcolonial theory that ignores the current history of Africa does not provide the appropriate contexts for such splendid works as Nadine Gordimer's *The Pickup* where she provides a rich reading of South African social history after Apartheid. Nor does it speak to the barbarism of tribal customs in Chinua Achebe's *Things Fall Apart* (1958) or the demagoguery of Idi Amin in the film *The Last King of Scotland* (Kevin Macdonald, UK, 2007; based on the 1998 novel by Giles Foden). I think of what an educated guide told me while I was visiting Mugabe's Zimbabwe—formerly Southern Rhodesia, one of the last colonies to become independent in Africa—"Colonialism was bad; this is worse." Or as Nicholas D. Kristof puts it, "The Belgians were brutal colonial masters in Congo, but after enduring subsequent rounds of kleptocratic incompetence and civil war, some Congolese feel nostalgic for the lesser tyranny of colonialism" ("Dinner with a Warlord").

I am hopeful that there will be more study of the intricacies of actual texts—narrators, structure, meaning—and more focus on relevant and urgent historical contexts. We can continue to repeat the same homogenizing bromides about neo-colonialism in Conrad's *Heart of Darkness* and *Nostromo* as well as Achebe's *Things Fall Apart* and Tim O'Brien's Vietnam novel *Going after Cacciato* (1978), or we can differentiate among the various histories of South American, African, and Asian countries.

With the awareness that domestic and foreign issues need thick readings, we should have less vague discussion linking the rise of post-modern theory with the end of colonization as if past modes of reading were a kind of imperialism. Indeed, as Marjorie Perloff has recently remarked: "Eurocentric theory has come to be seen less than adequate for dealing with the growing body of minority, transnational, and postcolonial literature" (Perloff 2007, 656). Certainly the gap between theory and facts in theorizing about Africa has opened the eyes of some scholars and led them back to a thicker reading of African history of the kind provided by Kristof's columns in the *New York Times*.

I am urging a return to a kind of rational thinking where synthesizing conclusions are cognizant of a thick reading of empirical facts, while discussions of literary texts focus on how narrative and recurring linguistic phenomena create meaning. I would hope that this new respect for facts be accompanied by awareness that not all perspectives are equally valid constructions, and that thus all deconstructions are not equally valid and that there are compelling readings that focus not on supposed gaps, fissures, and enigmas, but on the implications of dramatized human behavior. That is, concepts and generalizations about narrative and rhetorical strategies, and especially about themes and historical implications, will derive from a close reading of details. I would hope that the still-present mantra from the 1980s, "I hear what you are saying, *but*" followed by intuitive responses to a text that are really disguised political feelings, will take a back seat to discussion of what is going on within a text.

While not discounting the role of intuition and imagination in discovering relationships within texts and among texts, I am hopeful that we shall see some return to Enlightenment assumptions about the need for organizing knowledge and arguments in a rational way. Perhaps we will acknowledge that such a way of thinking is not obsolete Eurocentricism but a way of understanding the world beyond us.

We need to be more interested in the history of the practices of reading and writing in relation to cultural history and less in literary history as the evolution of forms. Yet it needs be said that such works as Ian Watt's *The Rise of the Novel* (1957) still provide a wonderful model for understanding forms in terms of social history, in this case the intellectual, social, and economic milieu of the eighteenth century.

In the future, I expect that fundamental anthropological and even neurological questions will be asked within the field of literary studies about why humans have the capability and desire to deal with fictional worlds and why we often do so in story form. We shall draw upon work now being done in cognitive studies and perhaps discover enhanced ways of reading. Our discussion of narrative will be more informed by the discoveries of science and we will be thinking more precisely about how memory works and more deftly about how we transmute memory into narrative.

We may learn—perhaps from this generation of graduate students—far more than we know now about which of our human needs are fulfilled by reading in silence about an imagined world even while belonging to a community of readers having a similar but often quite different experience. We may come to understand whether literature has an evolutionary function. When we do so, our defense of reading may be more precise and more eloquent.

Selective Bibliography

Achebe, Chinua. "An Image of Africa: Racism in Conrad's *Heart of Darkness*." *Massachusetts Review* 18 (1977); reprinted in *Heart of Darkness, An Authoritative Text, Background and Sources, Criticism*. 3rd ed. Ed. Robert Kimbrough, London: W.W. Norton and Co., 1988, pp. 251–61.

Booth, Wayne. *The Rhetoric of Fiction*. Chicago, IL: University of Chicago Press, 1961; rev. edn. 1983.

———. "The Rhetoric of Fiction and the Poetics of Fiction." *Novel* 1:2 (1968), 105–13.

———. *Now Don't Try to Reason with Me: Essays and Ironies for a Credulous Age*. Chicago, IL: University of Chicago Press, 1970.

———. *The Rhetoric of Irony*. Chicago, IL: University of Chicago Press, 1974.

———. *Critical Understanding: The Powers and Limits of Pluralism*. Chicago, IL: University of Chicago Press, 1979a.

———. "Ten Literal 'Theses.'" In Sheldon Sacks, ed. *On Metaphor*. Chicago, IL: Chicago University Press, 1979b.

———. "Between Two Generations: the Heritage of the Chicago School." *Profession* 82 (1982), 19–26.

Cavafy, Constantine P. *Collected Poems*. Trans. Edmund Keeley and Philip Sherrard, ed. George Savidis. Princeton, NJ: Princeton University Press, 1980.

Coetzee, J.M. "Awakening." *New York Review of Books* 50:16. October 23, 2003.

Cohen, Adam. "YouDebate: If Only the Candidates Were as Interesting as the Questioners." *The New York Times*. July 25, 2007.

Conrad, Joseph. *The Secret Agent*. New York: Penguin, 1963; orig. ed. 1907.

——. *The Secret Sharer*, ed. by Daniel R. Schwarz. Boston, MA: Bedford Books of St. Martin's Press, 1997.

Cooney, Terry A. *The Rise of the New York Intellectual: Partisan Review and Its Circle, 1934–45*, Madison, WI: The University of Wisconsin Press, 1986.

Culler, Jonathan. *Structuralist Poetics: Structuralism, Linguistics and the Study of Literature*. Ithaca, NY: Cornell University Press, 1975.

——. *The Pursuit of Signs: Semiotics, Literature, Deconstruction*. Ithaca, NY: Cornell University Press, 1981.

——. *On Deconstruction: Theory and Criticism after Structuralism*. Ithaca, NY: Cornell University Press, 1982.

Cunningham, Valentine. *Reading after Theory*. Oxford: Oxford University Press, 2002.

Delbanco, Andrew. "Academic Business." *The New York Times Magazine*. September 30, 2007.

Eagleton, Terry. *How to Read a Poem*. Oxford: Blackwell Publishing, 2007.

Edmundson, Mark. "The Risk of Reading." *New York Times Magazine*. August 1, 2004, 11–12.

Ehrenberg, Ronald G. *Tuition Rising: Why College Costs So Much*. Cambridge, MA: Harvard University Press, 2000.

Fiedler, Leslie. *Love and Death in the American Novel*, new rev. edn. New York: Dell, 1996.

Fish, Stanley. "Why We Built the Ivory Tower." *New York Times*. May 21, 2004.

——. "Tip to Professors: Just Do Your Job." *New York Times*. October 22, 2006.

Forster, E.M. *Aspects of the Novel*. New York: Harcourt Brace & World, 1954; orig. ed. 1927.

——. *A Passage to India*. Abinger Edition, ed. by Oliver Stallybrass. London: Edward Arnold; orig. ed. 1924.

Gordimer, Nadine. "The Arts in Adversity: Apprentices of Freedom." *New Society* (December 24, 31, 1981).

——. *The Pickup*. London: Penguin, 2001.

Gordon, Mary. "How Ireland Hid Its Dirty Laundry." *New York Times*. August 3, 2003.

Graff, Gerald. *Professing Literature: An Institutional History*. Chicago, IL: University of Chicago Press, 1987.

Guilory, John. *Cultural Capital: The Problem of Literary Canon Formation*. Chicago, IL: University of Chicago Press, 1993.

Howe, Irving. "Writing and the Holocaust." *The New Republic*. October 27, 1986, 27–39.

Jameson, Frederic. *The Political Unconscious: Narrative as a Socially Symbolic Act.* Ithaca, NY: Cornell University Press, 1981.

Joyce, James. *The Dead*, ed. by Daniel R. Schwarz. Boston, MA: Bedford Books of St. Martin's Press, 1994.

Keen, Andrew. *The Cult of the Amateur: How Today's Internet is Killing Our Culture.* New York: Doubleday, 2007.

Kellman, Steven C., and Irving Malin, eds. *Fiedler on the Roof: Essays on Literature and Jewish Identity.* Boston, MA: David R. Godfine, 1991.

Klingenstein, Susanne. *Jews in the American Academy: The Dynamics of Intellectual Assimilation 1900–1940.* New Haven, CT: Yale University Press, 1991.

———. *Enlarging America: The Cultural Work of Jewish Literary Scholars, 1930–1990.* Syracuse, NY: Syracuse University Press, 1998.

Klinkenborg, Verlyn. "Reading Thackeray's 'Vanity Fair' with the Illustrations Intact." *New York Times.* August 30, 2004, A18.

Kristof, Nicholas D. "Dinner with a Congolese Warlord." *New York Times.* June 18, 2007, A19.

Lang, Beryl, ed. *Writing and the Holocaust.* New York: Holmes and Meier, 1988.

Langer, Lawrence L. *The Holocaust and Literary Imagination.* New Haven, CT, and London: Yale University Press, 1975.

———. *Holocaust Testimonies: The Ruins of Memory.* New Haven, CT: Yale University Press, 1991.

Levinson, Marjorie. "What Is the New Formalism?" *Proceedings of the Modern Language Association* 122:2 (2007), 558–69.

Loesberg, Jonatan. *A Return to Aesthetics: Autonomy, Indifference, and Postmodernism.* Palo Alto, CA: Stanford University Press, 2005.

Miller, J. Hillis. *Fiction and Repetition: Seven English Novels.* Cambridge, MA: Harvard University Press, 1982.

Nafisi, Azar. *Reading 'Lolita' in Tehran: A Memoir.* New York: Random House, 2003.

Orwell, George. "Politics and the English Language." In *Essays.* New York: Doubleday Anchor, 1954, 162–77.

Pamuk, Orhan. "My Father's Suitcase." *The New Yorker.* January 1, 2007, 82–96, see 83, 90.

Perloff, Marjorie. "Presidential Address 2006: It Must Change." *Proceedings of the Modern Language Association* 122:3 (2007), 652–62.

Phelan, James. *Beyond the Tenure Track: Fifteen Months in the Life of an English Professor.* Columbus, OH: Ohio State University Press, 1991.

Phillips, Adam. "Art Ahead: Linger for a While, Look and Tell the Story." Review of Michael Kimmelman's *The Accidental Masterpiece: On the Art of Life and Vice Versa*. *The New York Times Book Review*, September 2, 2006, 30.

Reynolds, Mary. *Dante and Joyce*. Princeton, NJ: Princeton University Press, 1981.

Ricoeur, Paul. "The Model of a Text: Meaningful Action Considered as Text." *Social Research: Fiftieth Anniversary* 51:1 (1984), 185–218.

Rubin-Dorsky, Jeffrey, and Shelley Fishkin, eds. *People of the Book: Thirty Scholars Reflect on Their Jewish Identity*. Madison, WI: University of Wisconsin Press, 1996.

Said, Edward. *Orientalism*. New York: Vintage, 1978.

———. *Culture and Imperialism*. New York: Knopf. 1993.

Schemo, Diana Jean. "In Study Abroad, Gifts and Money for Universities." *New York Times*. August 13, 2007.

Schwarz, Daniel R. *The Humanistic Heritage: Critical Theories of the English Novel from James to Hillis Miller*. Philadelphia, PA: University of Pennsylvania Press, 1986.

———. *The Case for a Humanistic Poetics*. Philadelphia, PA: University of Pennsylvania Press, 1991.

———. *Reconfiguring Modernism: Explorations in the Relationship between Modern Art and Modern Literature*. New York: St. Martin's, 1997.

———. *Rereading Conrad*. Columbia, MO, and London: University of Missouri Press, 2001.

Soderholm, James. *Beauty and the Critic: Aesthetics in an Age of Cultural Studies*. Tuscaloosa, AL: University of Alabama Press, 1997.

Solomon, Andrew. "The Closing of the American Book." *New York Times*. July 10, 2004, 17.

Spieglman, Art. *Maus: A Survivor's Tale: My Father Bleeds History*. Vol. I. New York: Pantheon, 1986a.

———. *Maus: A Survivor's Tale: And Here My Troubles Began*. Vol. II. New York: Pantheon, 1986b.

Stone, Wilfred, *The Cave and the Mountain: A Study of E. M. Forster*. Palo Alto, CA: Stanford University Press, 1966.

Strier, Richard. "How Formalism Became a Dirty Word: and Why We Can't Do without It." In *Renaissance Literature and Its Formal Engagements*, ed. by Mark David Rasmussen. New York: Palgrave, 2002, 207–15.

Suleiman, Susan, and Inge Crossman, eds. *The Reader in the Text: Essays on Audience and Interpretation.* Princeton, NJ: Princeton University Press, 1980.

Theroux, Paul. *Dark Star Safari: Overland from Cairo to Cape Town.* New York; Houghton Mifflin, 2003.

Watt, Ian. *The Rise of the Novel.* Berkeley, CA: University of California Press, 1957.

Wood, James. "Ideas & Books." *Boston Sunday Globe.* August 15, 2004, D3.

Woolf, Virginia. *Mrs. Dalloway.* New York: Harcourt, Brace and World, 1925.

———. *To the Lighthouse.* New York: Harcourt, Brace and World, 1927.

———. *A Room of One's Own.* New York: Harcourt, Brace and World, 1929.

Index